Retreat Forward

One Woman's Journey Toward a More Authentic and Fulfilling Life

Stefanie D. Warren

re·treat (verb)
to withdraw, retire, or draw back,
especially for shelter or seclusion

for·ward (adjective)
directed toward a point in advance;
moving ahead; onward

Retreat Forward is the philosophy of
enabling personal growth (moving
Forward into deeper authenticity as
an individual) through prioritizing
relaxation, solitude, and reflection -
in other words, to *Retreat*.

PROJECT RETREAT FORWARD MISSION:

1. To circumnavigate this beautiful and amazing planet.

2. To gain knowledge and experience through living and working in intentional communities, retreat centers, and nature-focused destinations.

3. To enrich my life experience with new people and cultures, places, climates, flora, fauna, artwork, education, and adventures unknown!

PROLOGUE 1

PART ONE: Inspired Dreaming

Every Journey Begins with the First Step! 4
Pondering Travels of the Past 4
Making it Real 6
Fear...7
Embracing the World....................................10
Google Stalking..11
Full Circle 12
Privilege..14
And Now for Something Completely Different 16
Antici...pation 19
Breaking Up (with my job)..............................21
Choices..22
Letting Go 25
Gratitude and Love 27
Packing Light 28

PART TWO: Embracing the World

Day 1 - Mexico City 31
Day 2 - Mexico City Tour...............................32
Day 3 - Teotihuacan....................................33
Day 4 - Seeking Nature in the City.....................35
Day 6 - Morning in Cahuita, Costa Rica.................36
Day 6.5 - Grounded 37
Day 7 - I'm Melting!...................................38
Day 8 - Wildlife and the Wild Life 39
Day 9 - Chillin' in the Heat...........................40
Day 10 - A Walk en la Parque...........................42
Day 11 - Final Day in Cahuita..........................43
Day 12 - Tree House Hotel (La Fortuna).................44
Day 13 - La Fortuna Waterfall..........................44
Day 14 - Arenal Hanging Bridges 46
Day 15 - Arenal Volcano 47
Day 17 - Pura Vida 48
Day 19 - Waking up in Ollantaytambo, Peru 49
Day 20 - Cave of Bones.................................51
Day 21 - Shopping in Ollantaytambo 52
Day 22 - Getting High 54
Day 23 - Stormy 55

Day 24 - Machu Picchu 57
Day 26 - Body..58
Day 27 - Reflections on Peru 60
Day 28 - Intermediate Level (Brazil) 63
Day 29 - Missions Accomplished 65
Day 31 - On Board (Transatlantic)....................67
Day 32 - Rio de Janeiro 68
Day 34 - Battle of the Bed 70
Day 35 - Sea Dreams and Seaweed 72
Day 36 - Land Ho! 74
Day 37 - Imperium Neptuni Regis 75
Day 38 - The Middle of Nowhere.......................77
Day 39 - Social Nutrition 78
Day 40 - Bamboozled..80
Day 41 - Tenerife, Canary Islands 81
Day 43 - Reflections on the Cruise 82
Day 44 - Exploring Barcelona, Spain 85
Day 47 - Works of Gaudí 87
Day 49 - Reflections on Barcelona......................90
Day 51 - Morning in Italia (Italy) 91
Day 52 - Catacombs to Cupola 92
Day 53 - Dem Bones...95
Day 54 - When in Rome 96
Day 57 - Kissos, Greece 98
Day 61 - Meeting Needs 101
Day 64 - Change of Venue 104
Day 68 - Community.. 105
Day 71 - In Transit 108
Day 72 - Fish Food (Greece) 110
Day 74 - Reflections on Greece........................ 111
Day 76 - Arrival in India 114
Day 78 - Settling In 117
Day 79 - Free to Grow...................................... 120
Day 80 - Going Native....................................... 122
Day 81 - One Last Day at Greenex.................... 124
Day 82 - A Very Long Drive............................... 124
Day 83 - Currency Exchange............................. 125
Day 84 - Exploring Kuala Lumpur 126
Day 86 - MUD: The Musical............................... 129
Day 90 - Hey, Big Spender! (Indonesia)............ 131
Day 94 - Peace, Love, and Happines 133
Day 98 - The Red Center (Australia)................. 135
Day 100 - Treasure Hunt 137

Day 103 - Barossa Buzz 139
Day 106 - Campfire in the City 141
Day 107 - Jazz of Remembrance....................... 143
Day 109 - A Relative Unknown 144
Day 112 - Woods and Whiskies......................... 146
Day 114 - Night on the Town........................... 148
Day 120 - Bellbunya 150
Day 124 - A Different Pace............................... 152
Day 130 - Social vs...Solitude 154
Day 135 - Having Fun (New Zealand)................ 156
Day 138 - Black Water Rafting......................... 158
Day 144 - Te Papa 160
Day 147 - Reflections on Men........................... 162
Day 150 - Temporal Dynamics.......................... 164
Day 155 - Au Naturel (Hawaii).......................... 165
Day 160 - Uncle Robert's 167
Day 164 - Hot Lava... 169
Day 168 - Off Grid 171
Day 174 - Lavascape.. 172
Day 178 - Retreat Forward............................... 174

PART THREE: And Then...?

Home Day Three: Re-Entry 180
Home Day Fifteen: Time and Productivity 180
Home Month One: Finding My Way.................... 182
Home Week Six: Freedom................................. 184
Home Week Ten: COPE-ing 185
Home Week Fifteen: Solstice............................ 187
Home Week Seventeen: New Year 188
Home Week Nineteen: On the Hunt.................. 190
Home Week Twenty-Three: Awareness 192
One Year After Departure 195
PING! 196

PART FOUR: American Road Trip (A.R.T.)

Retreat Forward: A.R.T (American Road Trip) 200
Launching the Maiden Voyage 201
New Lifestyle 206
Plot Twist 208
Course Change.. 209
The Next Big Leap 211

Off-Roading 213
Boondocking 216
Safe Passage 217
Progress.. 219
Meet the Critters 221
The Boondocks.. 223
Civilization... 224
Interlude... 226
Day of Rest.. 227
Quartzsite - First Impressions 229
Rockin' in the Free World 231
Dental Tourism... 234
Moving Forward... 235
Whirlwind! 237
Waiting 239
I got it! 240
Preparations 242
Dreams and Visions 243

PART FIVE: The Refuge

Life 2.0 246
Upon Arrival 247
Meeting Jack.. 250
The Grove 251
Mud and Stress 253
Irons in the Fire 254
Win Some, Lose Some 256
Transformation... 258
Holding Pattern 260
Fear, Money, and Veggies................................. 261
EPIC 262
Debutante 264
Comparative Luxury... 265
Sanctuary.. 267
Power 269
A Beginning 271

PROLOGUE

Hi there! My name is Stefanie and this is my story.

The year was 2013 and I was 38 years old, living alone in my one-bedroom condo, spending most of my time and stress at my well-paying corporate job. I had all the comforts and conveniences of modern American life… and I was miserable.

I felt like running away, but I knew that nothing would be different if I was just living the same way in another place. I decided that if I was going to run, it needed to be toward something better, but I was just too tired and stressed to imagine any other lifestyle.

So I took a vacation, which led me to the Grand Canyon. Standing at the rim of the canyon, looking out into that vast and unfathomable natural beauty, I found my inspiration. I would travel the world to experience more of everything that this amazing planet has to offer. And in filling myself with a whole world's worth of inspiration… maybe I could dream up that better life I was seeking.

The story you're about to read is the blog I kept while planning the journey, traveling full circle around the planet, and returning home to find my way into a new life.

I hope you find inspiration, or at least entertainment, in my tale of personal transformation!

PART ONE:

INSPIRED DREAMING

Every Journey Begins with the First Step!
Sunday, March 22, 2015

While I've been saving money for my grand adventure over the last couple of years, I've also been researching alternate options. I've seriously considered delaying my travels so that I can buy an income property to provide myself with more financial security, but I've also been wondering just how long I can keep working in corporate America without doing lasting harm to my health and well being.

I've been pondering risks and rewards and just exactly what it is I want to do with my life - working up my courage to take a step away from the safety and comfort of "someday".

So this weekend I took a deep breath and made a commitment. I put my money where my dreams are, along with payment on one portion of my round-the-world trip!

Cruises tend to sell out the lower cost cabins early, so my first step was to book a 14-night Trans-Atlantic voyage from Brazil to Spain, departing just over a year from now.

My paternal grandfather crossed the equator by sea as as young man in the US Navy, earning himself a fanciful certificate featuring King Neptune with his trident and mermaids. Ever since I saw his awesome souvenir of that experience, I've wanted to do the same thing myself. This cruise will let me fulfill that equator-crossing wish!

The cruise isn't the first part of my trip or the last, but it's the first financial commitment, making my eventual departure delightfully and frighteningly real.

Travels of the Past
Friday, May 15, 2015

The first time I traveled without my family was on a school trip to Washington DC when I was 14 years old. That was also the first time I'd ever been on an airplane, which was very excit-

4

ing! My family's travel style was always long road trips to rural parts of the US with the five of us crammed into our beloved Caveman Camper.

At age 19 I moved to Chicago to pursue my dreams of life on the stage. I was soon cast in a play that was headed on a national tour – my first long term travel.

The cast and crew traveled together for about ten months. My fellow castmates packed everything they could carry and more, so I thought that my luggage of one large suitcase, plus a garment bag and a carryon backpack was light by comparison.

My bad packing habits continued into my first trips abroad in 2004 and 2005. In fairness, I was camping in a field for both of those trips and so things like sleeping bag and air mattress were necessities, but I did buy the largest wheeled duffel bag I could find and loaded it to the max. I only planned to drag it for short distances anyway. (Ha!)

Then I ended up unexpectedly in Glasgow, Scotland looking for a place to spend the night. Glasgow has hills to rival San Francisco - and I ended up dragging that ridiculously heavy bag up and down those hills far too many times as I got myself lost.

You would think that I learned my lesson in Glasgow, but on my next trip I packed that same heavy bag again, and went back to camp in that field in England. All went well, until I left camp and tried to walk a mile dragging my bag between bus stops… which is when the pull handle broke.

Fortunately, I was traveling with a friend at the time who was kind enough to hoist up one end of my bag while I held the other, as we hobbled that mile together. I finally learned my lesson and I haven't packed a heavy bag since!

In addition to most major US cities, my travels so far have taken me internationally to England, Scotland, Wales, Ireland, and Iceland; and in the USA to Alaska; Sedona, Arizona and the Grand Canyon; and to the Big Island of Hawaii.

It was when I was standing at the edge of the Grand Canyon, gazing out on that unfathomable beauty, that I was inspired to travel the world and experience much more of this amazing planet.

I've achieved a lot of dreams so far, but there's many more to go!

Making it Real
Sunday, May 03, 2015

Once I actually put down some money on this trip, I was eager to take more irreversible steps toward making my dreams reality. At my earliest opportunity, I talked with my manager at work. I had already mentioned my goals to him when I first started dreaming this a couple of years ago, but this time I gave him my firm departure date.

With that formality out of the way, I can now talk about my plans with friends at work. I'm really excited and spending a lot of my free time researching, so I tend to talk about these things.

I've also been reading a lot of RTW (round the world) travel blogs from others who have had – or are currently having – similar adventures. I had no idea there were so many people (families, couples, solos, and buddies) traveling around the world! Its reassuring to hear tales from so many other solo female travelers.

I signed up for a 30-day online course on RTW travel which has given me all sorts of good ideas, in addition to more handy spreadsheets!

On the advice of one of the many articles I've read about budgeting, I upped my budget buffer to 20%, which meant reducing some of my planned spending. My budget method is to find prices for travel and accommodations online, then round those prices up, and then use a spreadsheet to add the buffer on top of that.

My generously padded budget should help to cover unexpected expenses and make me feel good about saving money along the way. I tend to be frugal anyway, so this should help me justify buying and shipping home awesome souvenirs from time to time.

I still have a lot of saving to do in the next 314 days before my departure. Not only do I have my trip expenses to cover, but my mortgage and other basic monthly expenses back home while I'm gone. There's also the matter of supporting myself for some period of time after I return, while I figure out what to do next.

I can't imagine what to expect on this amazing journey, but I do know that I'll come out the other side changed and I'm going to need time to revise my post-trip lifestyle.

Fear
Saturday, May 23, 2015

So... Fear. I've been pondering writing about this topic for a while now, but fear is... well, y'know... scary.

Acknowledging your own fear means being vulnerable. It means admitting that at least part of you believes that you don't have what it takes to handle whatever you're contemplating. It means you're not perfect. It means you have weakness.

Yet Fear is an inescapable part of the human experience. Our bodies produce physiological symptoms of fear as a natural response to stimuli and our minds can't help but play along with the drama. With discipline we can train our minds and bodies to calm the symptoms of fear, but the experience can never be escaped entirely.

Setting off into the unknown by traveling is pretty scary on a number of levels. Home is one of my very favorite places to be and I'm going to be leaving it behind for a solid six months. There will be no running home because I forgot something important or because I'm stressed out and need the comfort of my personal refuge. I will be entirely cut off from one of my main sources of security.

I care very deeply about preserving my bodily comforts: sleeping well, eating foods that don't make me sick, enjoying a strong immune system, maintaining a comfortable bubble of personal space, understanding basic cultural expectations and social etiquette without a second thought. All of these things are at serious risk once I step outside of my usual routines.

Good bye, comfort zone! (I love you and I'll miss you!)

What if I can't communicate? What if my reservations get lost? What if *I* get lost?? What if I get tired and cranky and break down crying in some strange foreign place? What if somebody tries to assault me? What if something happens to someone I love back home while I'm gone? What if my identity gets stolen? What if I run out of money before I start working again? What if all of society collapses while I'm away and I can never return home??? (Fear and a fertile imagination are quite a potent combination.)

There are plenty of things that can go wrong over the duration of my trip. The best thing I can do with those fears is to follow them down the rabbit hole - in a productive way. What's the worst that could happen in any given scenario? And what could I do to get back on track if that were to happen? Then what can I do now to prepare, to make my life easier if the worst should happen?

Once I have those potential solutions I feel much more confident in my ability to handle whatever gets thrown my way, but logic and preparation only go so far in relation to Fear. Emotions aren't so easily tamed.

I've always been a highly emotional person and my relationship with Fear was intense from an early age. As a little girl, Scooby Doo was too scary for me because it involved things like ghosts and aliens. Ditto for E.T. and Star Wars. I was scared of fire and vampires - I still vividly recall childhood nightmares about both. I was never afraid of heights when climbing to the tops of tall trees, but carnival rides were terrifying.

At age 12, I had to take the emergency exit out of the Haunted Mansion ride at Disneyland because I was too scared. At age 15, I had to call my mom to come pick me up from a slumber party because they were going to watch Pet Sematary and I couldn't bear the thought of being in the same house with a scary movie.

I think it was the slumber party incident that was really the tipping point. I was tired of being limited by fear, so I decided to change that.

My first personal challenge was riding The Zipper - a carnival ride that turns you upside down. It was fun! Later that same year, I practiced facing my fears by jumping off of a 10-feet high cliff into a lake. Two years later, I had faced my fears to the point that I was ready to try skydiving. Moving my body outside of the plane and letting go was a very memorable moment of courage for me.

In my senior year of high school, the Vampire Lestat series of books by Anne Rice was very popular. I was still wary of filling my imagination with vampires, but I started reading that first book anyway. It was a great series and I went on to read about other "scary" topics.

At some point, fiction wasn't enough. I was craving exploration of the unknown, so I started studying parapsychology - allegedly factual occurrences of the same fictional topics that had scared me so badly as a child.

I came to accept that there's a lot of weirdness in this world, and that's OK. There is far more in existence than I will ever know, but I don't need to be scared in anticipation of encountering the unknown.

I guess what I'm saying is that facing my fears has been a passion of mine for most of my life. Traveling is scary. I have a whole bucket load of fears that I could easily pack along with me, but I really don't want to be weighed down by unnecessary baggage.

Its said that travel is a life changing experience, and it seems that even just preparing for travel can be a growth opportunity.

I can't get around Fear, but I can get through it.

Embracing the World
Wednesday, July 01, 2015

I just designed mini business cards with my website address on them so that I can easily share my blog with people I meet along the way. I chose to continue a theme on the cards that I started when I built my website: Embracing the World.

That simple phrase has a number of meanings for me. For one, I'll be literally encircling the planet - like wrapping my arms around a loved one. A really BIG loved one.

I love me some nature! I love the trees and the dirt and the plants and the animals - my adoration of the natural world is boundless. I want to hug Earth. I want to embrace the world - and traveling full circle is the best way I can think to do that.

Beyond the literal embrace is the aspect of acceptance. I live in my comfy little corner of world, surrounded by people who all share fairly similar lifestyles and outlooks. Even with all of our many, many differences, we're all still Americans. We don't recognize how similar we are because we're not aware of how different life can be.

I haven't spent time outside of the "Western World". I've never known much "different" in person, no matter how many documentaries I've watched or books I've read. But now I'm going out into the unknown (to me) world and one of my goals is to accept my experiences without judgment, which requires working past my unconscious assumptions and beliefs as I recognize them.

For example, the first time I saw one of Frida Khalo's self-portraits I was immediately fascinated... and kind of embarrassed to see her mustache in plain sight. Even though I believe myself to be a pretty accepting person, I caught myself wondering how those paintings were allowed to hang in public.

My American sensibilities were screaming that a mustache on a woman is a shameful thing. I'm aware of that subconscious feeling now, though I can't say that I've completely let it go yet. Unconscious beliefs can be tenacious, but the effort continues.

So... yea. Acceptance - not just of the experiences that stretch my boundaries, but also acceptance of my own limitations and weaknesses that are illuminated at the same time.

Embracing the World means embracing the uncomfortable challenges. Embracing the perceived failures. Embracing the accomplishment of simply moving my body from point A to point B.

And last, I expect that I'll be embracing a lot of the people I meet out there in the world. When traveling solo, I tend to develop bonds quickly with other travelers. Hugs are the inevitable result when parting - and meeting again!

So in this way I'll embrace the world, one new friend at a time.

Google Stalking
Monday, August 03, 2015

Some of the strengths that you might expect a world traveler to have would be a good sense of direction and accurate map reading skills. I am noticeably deficient in both qualities. This can make things a little stressful when trying to find my way to a destination in an unfamiliar location – let alone when the language around me is also unfamiliar! But this handicap can be mitigated with good preparation.

A few years ago, I started to "google stalk" each unfamiliar city before I traveled there. Google Maps is this awesome tool that will let you view nearly any accessible location on the planet, and in more populated areas, actually zoom down to a street view for a rotatable 360 degree image as if you were standing in the middle of the street looking around.

I can view my accommodations from afar so that I recognize the building when I get there in person. I can move the google camera down the street to trace the route I'll take from the bus stop, which is also conveniently indicated on the map. I can move over entire neighborhoods checking out restaurants, museums, attractions, conveniences... many with informative reviews linked to the map tags.

Google stalking enables me to know my way around instinctively as soon as I arrive in a new place. It's a great tool for the planning obsessed traveler!

Full Circle
Sunday, September 13, 2015

There are 180 days remaining until I depart home for my grand adventure around the world, and 180 is the same number of days over which I'll be traveling.

For those of you like me who like to play with numbers, you know that a full circle is divided into 360 degrees. So if you take those 180 days that I'll be traveling, and add them to the 180 days from now until departure, the result is 360 days of life. One full circle, as I imagine those days being degrees of time.

I often take time to ponder points one year, one full circle, forward and past in my life. Who was I at this time last year? How has my life changed? How do I envision my life at this time next year?

These questions are part of my spiritual practice of Druidry, as I maintain conscious awareness of the cycles of the natural world (the passing of seasons and the ever-changing aspects of nature) and how they relate personally to my life.

Druids observe each of eight points on the Wheel of the Year, honoring the high and low points of the Summer and Winter Solstices, the balance of day and night at the Spring and Autumnal Equinoxes, and the cross-quarter days between each of those four points.

Today is little more than a week before the Autumnal Equinox. This is the time when the lighter half of the year is passing, and we're moving towards the darkness of winter. Emotional currents shift along with the waning light and warmth.

The light-hearted joy of summer trip planning gives way to the more grounded thoughts of health, safety, and preparing for contingencies along the way. The desire to run free out in the warm and gentle world slowly becomes the desire to snuggle up cozily indoors, protected from the colder, harsher realities of nature.

I crawl into my bed each night - my awesome organic locally-made comfy yet firm latex mattress set that I dearly love, with my soft flannel sheets and supportive pillows - and then I think about sleeping in hostels.

I think about questionable bed linens, lumpy mattresses, noisy nights, unfamiliar scents, and how hard it is for me to sleep away from home. I think about the slim chance of sleeping on planes, buses, and trains. I think about how cranky I get without enough sleep after only one night...

But then I also think about being in a tree house in a jungle, surrounded by those strange and mysterious night noises, and by the warm breezes passing through my cozy oasis in the trees. I think about being in a little shack on the edge of a tropical black sand beach, hearing the waves crashing and the birds calling. I think about opening my eyes in the morning and seeing an expansive view of ancient temple ruins from my bed.

There's a part of me that feels the call towards winter hibernation – hunker down at home and settle in for the long haul. But the rest of me knows that the light will return, and with it my desire to go back out and discover the world.

I still need to travel halfway around a year before I can travel full circle around the world. Two more seasons must pass before my departure.

The Wheel of the Year will be at the opposite point from now – turned 180 degrees - looking forward into the lighter half of the year when I depart, but first, I must walk through the dark half of the year that is only just beginning.

It seems appropriate that my travels will be headed east into the rising sun, straight into the light of day. Because the only way to reach the day, is to keep on going through the night.

Privilege

Saturday, October 24, 2015

You're so lucky! I'm so jealous! I want to go too!

I've been hearing those comments a lot lately in regards to my plans, and I understand the envy because I've been there myself many times.

Nearly twenty years ago I remember being intensely envious of a friend who described his months of bumming around Scotland – making friends, hanging out in pubs, hiking and having adventures. This same friend then went on a road trip for months around the US.

How does anybody manage to do things like that??

At that time, I was in college and working a few part-time jobs. I was selling my blood plasma as often as they'd let me, getting paid for psych experiments, and considering selling my own eggs.

I was living paychecks to paychecks and could hardly afford to take a sick day, let alone take off months with travel expenses to boot. But my friend's travels were always in the back of my mind, seeding a dream that I desperately wanted to follow.

Time went on and I surrendered to the siren song of stable higher income, taking a desk job with benefits. After a year, I was ecstatic to enjoy my first ever one-week paid vacation. I celebrated by driving my T-top Camaro (oh yea) down the Pacific coast to California and back.

More time passed and my desire for international travel began to grow. Having several years of stable employment and my debt under control by then, I planned my first trip abroad to the UK.

It was fortunate that I was already planning a budget trip (made affordable by camping for two weeks) because I got laid off only six weeks before my departure.

There was no way I was going to cancel my trip just because I lost my job! I went on the trip as planned and fell in love with the land, the people, and the freedom of being away from the usual business of making a living.

Rather than find another job when I returned from my trip, I decided to go back to university to finish the degree I had started ten years earlier. For the next two years I had full time classes and part time work, leaving me with almost no down time and definitely no "extra" income - already swimming in student loans.

Yet in the summer between those two years of university, I went back to the UK. I didn't have the money – the whole trip was charged to my credit card – but I had to go. The pull to travel was too strong to resist.

After graduation I found an entry-level corporate job and started working my way into more responsibility and better salary. Over nine years working for the same company I've been able to take four more trips to the UK, pay off my student loans and other debts, and save up for this grand journey of mine.

I haven't gotten married or paid for a wedding. I haven't gotten divorced or had to split up my assets. I haven't had babies or the expenses that go along with kids. I haven't bought the latest technologies. I haven't subscribed to expensive services. I haven't had any medical issues requiring expensive intervention. I haven't had to financially support family members in need.

Yea – I'm definitely lucky. I will never deny that and I'm grateful every day for the health and freedom that I enjoy in this world, but I've also made conscious choices to bring myself to this result.

I could have made different choices if anything else was more important to me, but the truth is... exploration and experience are the most important things to me. Being part of the wonders that this amazing world has to offer is what matters to me, and so my choices reflect those values.

As an American citizen, I recognize that I'll enjoy a lot of privilege in the world. US passports are offered easy entry into many countries, while the passport holders of many other nations must undergo more rigorous scrutiny. I'll be largely relying on people who have learned English as a second language as I travel – another privilege of the western world. My fair skin and blonde hair will set me apart as an income-generating tourist in many rural areas, leading to deferential treatment in my favor.

There's no denying that I'm indeed very privileged. I can only practice deep gratitude and do my best to spread the joy of my good fortune out into the world, in the hopes that others may be inspired to find their own joys and great fortunes.

And Now for Something Completely Different
Saturday, November 28, 2015

Most of us have many little routines that propel us through daily life. We repeat the same rituals of maintenance at regular intervals: eat, bathe, work, chores, socialize, sleep. Sometimes we flow mindlessly along in these rhythms, solely focused on keeping up with the beat, forgetting than anything else could possibly matter.

I'm no different. The repeating rhythms of my days and weeks are a source of comfort and security. I know what to expect from day to day and I've been doing this for a while, so I've got my routines well-honed for maximum efficiency. It's so much easier to operate on autopilot than to make conscious choices about everything all the time.

Our routines can become so ingrained that they become part of our identities. In my teens and 20s, I was a definite "night person". My preferred sleeping hours were 2am-10am. Even the thought of starting work before 11am just seemed so uncivilized.

And yet that identity has distinctly shifted for me over the years and I'm now a "morning person", which is something the younger me could have never imagined. These days, my body is wide awake around 5:30am, and ready to sleep before 10pm.

I'd love to sleep in, but no matter how tired I am when I wake, my body is ready to rise with the sun. That works well for my current lifestyle, making getting to the office by 7am every morning manageable.

But here's the thing... I'm about to change my rhythm dramatically. Most of the time I'll get to sleep during the night, and I'm sure that I'll eat at more or less regular intervals, but that's about it for routine as I travel.

There have been very few and brief times in life when I've had that sort of flexibility of schedule. Who knows if I'll end up a morning person or a night person when I have no daily routine driving my sleep habits?

The longest I'm staying anywhere is two weeks, which is almost enough time for my body to acclimatize to daily cycles, but not quite. I won't have the chance to develop habits in my environment, which should allow for some interesting observations.

I'd prefer to avoid any connection to the over-clichéd "find yourself" genre of travel writing, but who am I kidding? I'm eager to know who I am out there - away from my comfort zone, away from the familiar, away from the expectations of anyone who has known me before.

I'm eager to know what I'm going to learn through new experiences, and how that will affect the person I am today. And that does sound suspiciously like finding myself.

One of the enduring mysteries of psychology is Nature versus Nurture. Are we born as distinctly formed personalities, or are we born as infinite potentials to be shaped by our environment and interactions? I'm looking forward to exploring that question more on a personal level, as I leave all of my usual Nurture behind (home, family, friends, job, community, etc.) and let my Nature roam free into new experiences.

But it's no easy thing to simply "let go" of who I've known myself to be for the last forty years. Throughout the process of planning for this world adventure, I've come upon any number of mental brick walls that previously prevented me from considering certain possibilities.

So many times I had the conversation with myself, "I can't do that!"… "Well, why not?"

My reasons were generally based in fears and prejudices, which aren't valid reasons and therefore had to be let go. I'm still in that process, clearing out the many subconscious assumptions that keep me from understanding the world (and myself) better.

This quote from Marcus Garvey (paraphrased by Bob Marley) has profound meaning and deeply relates to the process I'm living: *"Emancipate yourselves from mental slavery, none but ourselves can free our minds!"*

There is strong pressure from society and well-meaning folks to be a part of the system. Keep that "good job" that gives you a sanctioned way to spend your days. It's really the only way to get affordable health care and, if you're lucky, a few weeks every year in which to live your dreams outside of work obligations.

It's crazy to quit your career and leave your life behind, but it's also an effective way to break out of your own mental prison. If you stop playing the game - **stop accepting what you're told should be important to you** - it's possible to discover what actually matters to you.

Right now, I don't know how much of myself is ME and how much is a construct of the society in which I live. I recognize some of my distinctly American beliefs from my travels and friendships in the UK, but I haven't experienced enough perspective on the world yet.

I am lovingly held in a web of family, friends, and community… all of whom have beliefs about who I am, how the world works, and how things should be. This is the normal condition of humanity, and those inter-relationships are undeniably a powerful shaping force on every individual – good, bad, and otherwise.

However, I'll be separated from those shaping forces for months, and their influence on me will lessen over the distance. As I travel, new influences will be introduced, and gone again shortly after making an impact. New experiences will color my perception of everything that comes after.

With each new destination, each new human connection, and each new spectacle of natural beauty - my capacity to understand and relate to the world will grow.

There is life as I have always known it, and then there is every other possibility in this huge and varied world of ours.

And soon (105 days to departure), it will be time for me to try something completely different!

Antici...pation
Friday, December 11, 2015

Lately I've been thinking a lot about anticipation. I've been planning this trip for nearly three years, putting immense amounts of time and energy into research and logistics. This is entirely a labor of love and has generated an ongoing current of passionate hope and joy in my life. I've been riding high for many months now, just on the very IDEA of my upcoming freedom and adventure.

That has me pondering anticipation on a smaller scale as well. Like so many people, I work a pretty standard Monday to Friday schedule with weekends off. I've noticed that I feel my best – most joyful and hopeful and free – on Fridays. The good feelings start before I even leave the office, as colleagues all around me are caught in the same increasing wave of joyful anticipation.

There's an entire genre of internet memes devoted to "hump day" on Wednesdays, and the celebration of inching closer to the weekend. Pop culture acknowledges that Mondays are always the worst, being farthest away from the next weekend. Strangely, instead of being refreshed after two days away from work, the leisure we've just enjoyed is forgotten by Monday morning and we're focused on anticipating the next opportunity for freedom.

So it seems to me that anticipation is a pretty powerful force. The happiness that I feel in anticipation of my journey is real. Even if

I never again step outside of my front door (highly unlikely), I've already experienced so much joy in my envisioned travels.

And the really cool thing...? All of that joy comes from within me. There's no external force creating or allowing my happiness - it's all generated by my own thoughts and actions.

But like any powerful force, anticipation can be used for evil just as easily as it can be used for good. It's easy to let our minds fall into cycles of dread, so that anticipation weighs us down in every moment.

So many times, I've found myself with an unpleasant task in the future, and then spent days and nights thinking about it, (unnecessarily) worried and miserable in anticipation. So many times, I've put up my guard in anticipation of a conflict, while my mind plays through every possible horrible scenario. So many times, I've created my own suffering through anticipation.

I guess what I'm saying is that I need to become a Jedi Master of the Force of Anticipation. (Does that come with a light saber?)

Life is going to continue on after I return home from my grand adventure. Its very possible to suffer a big dip in good vibes once I'm back in "the real world" and burdened with the basic responsibilities of adulthood again.

Perhaps then I can use my Jedi powers to craft a new dream filled with joyful anticipation to sustain me into an unknown future...

Breaking Up (with my job)
Saturday, December 19, 2015

Running off to have adventures is all well and good, but it means leaving a lot of my current life behind to do it, including my job. For the last nine years I've held a variety of positions in the same company. Like most long-term relationships, it was great in the beginning.

Loyalty and dedication are very much a part of my nature, and I was devoted to the company for many years. The choices I made in life put my job first. In return, the job supported me financially with a regular paycheck, socially with the deep connections I made with my coworkers, and personally with many challenges that required/inspired me to grow and develop.

Over the years, both the company and I have changed. You might say that we've grown apart. We no longer have the same goals and values, but we've been through a lot together. Part of me really wants to stick around to work it out. I've invested so much of myself in the company, and I hate to abandon the people who have come to depend on me.

But the fact remains that things really have changed. Every day I recognize that I'm spending so much of my time and effort on goals that aren't my own. I care deeply about my work because that's my nature, but I feel that making the company's goals my priority in life is simply not in integrity with who and what I am.

And so the only healthy choice is to move on.

No matter how sure I am of making the right choice for me (and I'm very sure!), I find that it's still a very emotional decision. Even though I'm just leaving my job, not breaking up with a romantic partner, somehow my emotional state feels remarkably similar.

A couple of days ago I had a meeting with management to discuss the future of my current position. There was nothing surprising in the meeting and I generally agreed with all of the plans for transitioning a new person into my role. And yet... I found myself holding back tears for the rest of the day.

I received praise and thanks for my contributions to the company, but my emotional response was only deeply disappointed that I hadn't been begged to stay.

I truly don't **want** to stay, and I honestly don't want to have to say no if they had asked me to stay, and still I was crushed that they hadn't asked. That kind of twisted emotional logic is something I've only experienced with romantic breakups before.

So I guess that the company and I are in that awkward stage of breaking up. There are things that we still need to do together. We're still living in the same house, the routine still feels like normal, but we're slowly moving our things out little by little and change hangs in the air. We have another two and a half months of this before my last day.

In order to Embrace the World, I first have to let go of what I'm still holding on to…

Choices
Saturday, January 30, 2016

If there's one thing that I've gained a lot of experience with in planning this trip so far, it's making choices. I started from scratch – no template, no model, no example I was trying to follow – just the entire planet and a reasonable budget to make my way around it. The where, when, how, what… every single choice has been mine alone to make.

Making choices is something that we all do every day, and our choices can be influenced by an infinite number of factors. I remember a movie from the late 90s called Runaway Bride. Julia Roberts played a woman with a pattern of accepting marriage proposals, only to leave her grooms abandoned at the altar. A pivotal scene in the movie occurs when Roberts' character realizes that she has no idea how she likes her eggs prepared, because her choice always defaults to whatever type of eggs her partner prefers. She then begins a quest to determine exactly which kind of eggs she truly likes, in a journey of self-discovery.

It seems that a lot of us don't know how we like our eggs, so to speak. We make choices based on what we think is expected of us, or on what some perceived authority has declared is correct. We make choices even when we believe that we have no choice, focused on one possibility to the exclusion of all others.

Recently I've been pondering a major change to part of my trip, so I reviewed my Mission. I know that my focus tends to shift over time, and so I wrote a mission statement for Project Retreat

Forward at the very beginning, to remember what I set out to do in the first place.

Number two on my list states that my mission is: to gain knowledge and practical experience through living and working with intentional communities, retreat centers, and other nature focused destinations.

One of my dreams is to live and work in an intentional community, so developing relationships with communities is very important to me. I submitted my application to a retreat center in Hawaii to join their sabbatical program for the final month of my journey, but was told that the program was on temporary hold, so I started looking for a contingency plan.

I found a gorgeously simple off-grid cabin on three private jungle-covered acres near the retreat center, which I can rent for a month (along with the owner's Smart Car) for well within my budget. The allure of my own little private slice of jungle paradise (complete with outdoor lava rock shower) to enjoy while I reflect on the many experiences of my journey... well, that just sounds like too much bliss to pass up.

But I've been struggling against the idea that I wouldn't be honoring the commitment of my mission if I don't prioritize developing community relationships. It seems to me that I should **want** to put community above any other choice, and yet... my feelings tell me quite clearly that my true desire, at least at this time, is the choice of jungle solitude.

And then I looked back at my mission: "...and other nature-focused destinations."

I love the little jungle cabin not just for its charm and setting, but for its sustainability. The rainwater catchment system supports the kitchen, as well as the outdoor shower and toilet. The cabin is powered by solar panels. The owner built some of the furnishings himself and stays there often to maintain the house and garden. There's a lot to learn living in such a place, and that qualifies as a nature-focused destination.

It's good to know that changing my choice is still in alignment with my original mission, but this process is helping me learn that listening to my feelings is the best guidance system.

No matter what I may think is right for me, my feelings have final say on the matter. (Its feelings that will keep you up all night and distract you all day.) I don't always understand my feelings, especially not at first, but the more I listen, the better I get at making good choices.

Many different spiritual practices aim to quiet outside distractions to allow for hearing "that still small voice within." For me, I think, that small voice speaks not in words, but in sensations.

Whether I purposefully tune into them or not, those sensations are with me in every moment of every day. When I make a good choice, I feel light and unencumbered. When I make a bad choice, I feel heavy and uncomfortable. But of course, it's never quite as simple as good or bad – life is complex, and feelings are even more so.

I suppose that's the skill to be honed: listening to that inner voice, learning to understand it, then to trust it. And finally, using that guidance to inform my choices.

I'm learning to embrace myself from the inside out, so that I can embrace the world.

Letting Go
Wednesday, February 17, 2016

I'm trying to let go. I need to let go, because the time to be gone is drawing ever closer. It's so hard, because there is so much of my life – people, projects, relationships, goals, interests – which I have to set aside when I'm no longer physically here. I care deeply about all of that/them, and I have to let it all go in order to remove myself for six months (or longer).

I've planned, oh how I've planned, for every minute detail that you could imagine. I've double-checked, triple-checked, and obsessed over every tiny thing – and still I found a glaring error a few days ago.

The quick and easy last-minute electronic visa to enter India that I had planned on, is only acceptable at certain airports – not including the one I'm already booked to fly into. (Ack!)

Now here I am – 23 days from departure – and my passport is not in my possession. (Ack!) I sent it to an agency in San Francisco to take my ginormous application packet to the Indian embassy and get a very expensive (all fees included) tourist visa, which is good for my entry point in Kozhikode.

If all goes well, I'll have my passport back a few days before I leave. Wow, are my nerves not good with that tight margin of error, but it was the best option and I took the chance.

I gave very advanced notice to my job that I'd be leaving (a year ago) and a few reminders since then, but the corporate wheels turn slowly. I have just over two weeks left on the job and they haven't hired a replacement for me yet. Despite all my best efforts and intentions, I won't be around by the time my replacement starts, and I won't be able to offer any personal training.

And so now here I am – twelve business days away from leaving my job – and all I can do is write up procedures and try to share my knowledge about special projects with coworkers to pass on after I'm gone. I wanted to provide for a smoother transition, but my powers are limited.

If you haven't noticed… planning is kinda my thing. I enjoy it, I'm good at it, and I tend to rely heavily on it. But the thing about plans, as anyone who has ever planned can tell you, is that they're not guaranteed to work out exactly as expected.

I'm sitting with a lot of anxiety at this point of transition in my life and find myself clinging desperately to my plans. "How can that visa problem be true? I *planned* for it, don't you understand??"

So I take a deep breath… and let it go. (*Repeat as necessary*)

I know that not all of my plans will work out. I don't know what's going to happen, but the odds are in favor of unexpected circumstances. I'm going to have to roll with it and improvise when these things happen – or maybe even suffer for a little while.

I have choices in how I respond to everything that transpires along the way. I can get upset, or I can chill and look for the value in the adventure. The chances of me being in physical peril are pretty slim (knowing my fondness for keeping out of harms' way), so I'll probably just have to deal with varying levels of discomfort and inconvenience. Not fun, but nothing I can't actually handle.

So I'll take a deep breath… and let it go. (*Repeat as necessary*)

With each twinge of regret about missing people and events while I'm away, I'll take a deep breath and let it go. With each twinge of sadness at the anxiety my adventures cause to my loved ones, I'll take a deep breath and let it go. With each twinge of guilt about leaving my work community behind with a mess, I'll take a deep breath and let it go.

I'll just keep breathing, and keep letting it go, and it's all gonna be OK. And now I leave you with this quote from one of Middle Earth's favorite adventurers:

"We are plain quiet folk and have no use for adventures. Nasty disturbing uncomfortable things! Make you late for dinner! I can't think what anybody sees in them." ~Bilbo Baggins

Gratitude and Love
Wednesday, March 02, 2016

Nine days until departure. Two days until I leave my job. Wow.

It feels surreal and I can't quite wrap my head around the undeniable fact that my life isn't going to continue exactly as it's been going for so many years now. I feel like I'm getting ready to leap from a moving train. I know that no matter how carefully I plan and calculate, the impact from that leap is going to hurt some.

And as I'm preparing to leap, to leave, to change and grow… I am receiving SO much love and support. Almost daily, people tell me they're finding inspiration in my project. I never anticipated how much my journey would impact others, especially just from vicarious involvement! I really do feel like I'm taking an entire community of people along with me for the ride, and I can't wait to tell you all about it.

There's something very powerful in being heard. It can be so hard to speak from your authentic voice in daily life. Everybody is busy, rushing from one thing to the next, rarely any time to stop and truly connect with another person. "How are you" becomes a rhetorical question in passing, rather than a genuine concern. Questions that really matter are considered somehow taboo in polite company.

In this forum, I'm very open about my thoughts and feelings. I make myself vulnerable in that way as a conscious choice in this huge process of change. I'm striving to create a more authentic life for myself through all of this, and the best way I know how to do that is to pour my heart and soul out onto these pages to share with all of you.

You are my witness in this grand journey, and you have my eternal gratitude. Thanks for reading and thanks for caring!

One can never be alone when there is one other listening.

Packing Light
Thursday, March 10, 2016

The question keeps coming up… what do you pack for six months around the world? First of all, I've traveled enough by now to learn that packing light is a virtue in almost every circumstance. Second, I feel more secure if I can keep my baggage within eyesight and know that we will arrive at my destination together, so my goal is to pack as light as possible and avoid checking anything!

I chose a rolling carry-on as my main bag and an anti-theft shoulder bag for my tablet and other easy-access items. A radio frequency-protected wallet with detachable cross-body strap rounds out my luggage.

My travel wardrobe is designed to allow for lots of different outfits from only a few basic pieces, with every piece following a palette of compatible colors. I prefer blending to sticking out when I travel, so I chose muted colors and styles. I can get away with a bare minimum of clothing since I plan on doing a little laundry at least once a week.

Going full circle around the world means encountering some extreme environments. I'll go from the sweaty green jungles along the tropical beaches of Costa Rica, to the high-altitude mountains of Peru. I'll go from the sultry monsoons of Southeast Asia to the depths of winter in Australia. I'll go from manual labor in farming and construction, to formal nights on a cruise ship. Functionality of every piece is key.

I did a lot of research into technical clothing – items designed to be lightweight, water-resistant, bug-resistant, etc. I pared down my list to the bare essentials, assuring that I can comfortably carry everything I need with me.

Until I find things along the way that I just can't resist, but hey, I packed light so there's room for more!

My bags are packed and the only thing left to do is... GO!

PART TWO:

EMBRACING THE WORLD

Day 1 - Mexico City
Saturday, March 12, 2016

Both of my flights (Seattle to Phoenix, then to Mexico City) were uneventful, and I even managed to complete the Spanish language version of the customs form.

I connected with my pre-paid taxi at the Mexico City airport and enjoyed the... exhilarating ride to my hostel. In the US, we like our roads nice and tidy with lines that drivers mostly stay within, but Mexico apparently prefers their traffic more free form.

My hostel appears to be a pretty happening place with shops and restaurants in the courtyard lobby. There's also a cozy bar in the back near the hostel guest entrance, which is where I sit right now enjoying a nice cold Corona.

My private room could best be described as... spartan. I was given a single sheet and towel at check in. There are two bare single beds, one small waste basket, and two hooks on the wall. (Maybe I'll just call that pleasingly minimal.)

It was a lovely warm evening so I went out to explore. The entire city has the feel of a street fair. I followed my ususal rule of thumb when out in the world: If you hear live music, find it!

I followed the sounds of a drum and bugle corps to Placa de Constitucion in the center of the historical district, then I wandered around the huge public square, people watching and checking out vendors.

The stores in this city don't have doors. It appears that they just roll up the front wall of each store, lending to the street fair atmosphere. In addition to the brick and mortar shops, the streets are lined with vendors laying out their wares on tarps and blankets, selling everything from USB storage, to purses, to kids toys.

And of course, street food! I enjoyed some excellent street tacos for dinner.

I'm getting the impression that Mexico is much more romantic than the USA. I noticed half a dozen men waiting with bouquets of roses in the airport, and lots of hand holding and kissing everywhere in public. It's really lovely.

Day 2 - Mexico City Tour
Sunday, March 13, 2016

Today was the walking city tour, which meant negotiating crowds. We started at the noteworthy Museum of Anthropology, which illustrates the history of civilization in the Mexico region for as far back as anybody knows.

The tour continued in the Zocalo area, with a very long line for entrance to the National Palace (home of el Presidente) to view the extensive murals painted by famed Mexican artist, Diego Rivera.

Being a government building, the Palace is guarded by military police in full uniform, carrying combat weapons. There is no shortage of law enforcement around here, with at least two police officers on every corner. Many establishments have private security guards with very large guns at the ready.

We wandered on down the main street of Zocalo, frequently dodging aggressive panhandlers and organ grinders asking for change. There are also lots of costumed figures along the main avenue, who charge for posing with them for photos. This is obviously a high-tourist area.

The tour ended at the Museo de Bellas Artes (beautiful art!), which was broadcasting a recorded opera on a big screen outside. My feet insisted on a bit of a rest before I continued my endless wandering, so I chilled out in my room for a bit before going out in search of dinner.

I definitely felt some trepidation about finding a restaurant. I don't know the protocol! Do I walk in a take a seat? Do I go up to the bar? Will the check come to the table? Do I have to tip? What if we can't understand each other?

Eventually, I bit the bullet and went in to a restaurant/bar that had an appealing menu in the window and a casual vibe. I walked in and was seated at my table for one.

It took me a moment to understand that the waiter was asking me what I want to drink - and I know better than to ask for my usual water! He suggested juice, so that was my choice - orange juice and steak medallions for dinner.

I enjoyed the meal and left a tip. Whether it's expected or not, I appreciated that the waiter did his best to speak English to me. I found a place still open to buy a couple of bottles of water, and now I'm all set for my early morning tour tomorrow.

Day 3 – Teotihuacan
Monday, March 14, 2016

Today was the tour of Teotihuacan, a pre-Aztec city with many step-style pyramids. Upon arrival at the city, our first climb was up the temple of Quetzacoatl - the feathered serpent god.

More than 100 human sacrifices were made in building the temple. We're told that extended family groups would choose one member as a sacrifice to the temple, protecting the remaining family members from being sacrificed.

We continued on down the 2km Avenue of the Dead, the main street of the city that sprawls out from around the central grouping of temples. As we walked, we learned about their system of transporting water through the city and into the main central pool. Bathing was very important to the people, as a means of purification prior to sacrifices.

At last we came to the Temple of the Sun, which had been looming in the distance all along. The pyramid has an intimidating 265 extremely steep and uneven steps leading to the top. Those of us with enough stamina set out to scale the stairs and were rewarded with incredible views in all directions.

After more walking, we came to the Temple of the Moon, a considerably smaller structure, but presiding over a plaza where we're told many ceremonies and sacrifices took place. This place felt sacred to me, and I took the opportunity to walk the perimeter of the platform, greeting the spirits of the place as I went.

The steps of the Moon pyramid were each 18-24 inches high, and made for a challenging climb. We were only able to access the mid-level of this pyramid due to the upper steps being blocked off after a fatal accident several months ago. (I'm telling you, those steps are treacherous!)

By the time the tour ended my body was utterly exhausted from the walking, climbing, heat and sun. I was eager to return to my hostel for a rest, but then our bus encountered Mexico City rush hour. Rather than sit in traffic for another hour, I opted to hop off the bus and walk the remaining mile back to my hostel, despite my exhaustion.

I collapsed into my hostel bed and read a book for a while, before my endless wanderlust returned and I dragged my tired bones out into the city once more. There are as many ice cream shops in Mexico City as there are Starbucks in Seattle, so I just enjoyed a refreshing scoop of lemon sorbet before finally losing my stamina and heading back to the hostel.

Day 4 - Seeking Nature in the City
Tuesday, March 15, 2016

On my final day in Mexico City I set out to explore Chapultepec Park, one of the largest city parks in the Western hemisphere. The first section of the 1,700 acre grounds I explored was filled with gorgeous purple-flowering jacaranda trees, which seemed utterly whimsical in comparison to the grit of the city.

Taking a Turibus to discover other areas of the immense park, I found a zoo with free entry and wandered through the exhibits. The zoo animals were beautiful, but the little native lizards darting across the paths were my real favorites.

On the return Turibus, I found myself once again in rush hour traffic. Have I mentioned how much I really hate traffic? As soon as I saw a familiar landmark, I jumped off the bus and power-walked my traffic frustration away in the mile back to my hostel.

I've really loved my visit to Mexico City - the architecture is so elaborate and the people are so beautiful and friendly. However, within 24 hours of arrival I started developing a deep chest cough, and my sinuses aren't in much better condition. I've seen a number of people walking around with surgical masks and now I understand why.

I'm starting to feel desperate for some clean fresh air and I can hear the lush green jungles of Costa Rica calling to me...

Day 6 - Morning in Cahuita, Costa Rica
Thursday, March 17, 2016

I arrived at my destination on the Caribbean coast of Costa Rica after dark last night, exhausted from a very long day of travel. I went to bed not long after, hoping for a long restful sleep to help get my sinuses over doing their impression of Mexico City traffic (totally congested).

However, I found that the jungle rises early and I laid in bed this morning in a semi-conscious state listening to the noises of the creatures waking up around me.

The rooster was first on the scene around 3:30am - he obviously didn't get the memo about daylight savings time. Next came the gentle chorus of of bird song. As I was drifting back to sleep to the peaceful music of nature, I heard an odd low rumble start and quickly crescendo into a loud roar-like sound that I had never heard before.

It sounded like a hungry Godzilla outside my bedroom window, or maybe the sound of an angry spirit released as the ancient stone door of a cursed temple is rolled open after millennia.

And yet, the peaceful birdsong continued and my cabin kitty was obviously undisturbed. Assuming that meant that whatever monster lurked outside was no threat, I went out to investigate.

There was nothing to be seen past the tall walls of foliage surrounding our little complex of cabins. Then it dawned on me (pun intended)... howler monkeys live in Costa Rica! With that mystery solved, and the monkeys finished greeting the day shortly thereafter, I was able to drift back into a sweaty sleep.

I've never experieced a tropical climate before. The air is amazingly dense, hot, and damp. I can feel the thick green oxygen flushing the Mexican smog out of my lungs with each breath. Even though I packed mostly for warm/hot weather, everything I brought makes me feel totally overdressed.

I can hear the nearby ocean waves crashing as I sit here on my

patio writing this, and I'm compelled to go greet the Caribbean...
after liberal application of sunblock, of course.

Day 6.5 – Grounded
Thursday, March 17, 2016

While I would love to continue blaming my congestion and cough
on Mexico City, I have to finally admit that I have a cold. Drat. So
to give my body the rest it needs, I grounded myself. No adventuring today!

After my howler monkey wakeup call this morning, I enjoyed the
specialty breakfast of the house – banana pancakes with mixed
tropical fruit. Oh baby, was that good food! I took a short walk
down the road to wade in the Caribbean for a few minutes, then
retired to my cabin for the rest of the day to lounge in a hammock,
swaying in the breeze and reading a book.

When the hottest part of the day had passed, I remembered that
a body needs more than just rest, and set out to find some food.
I can hear the music of the nearby reggae bar from my cabin, so
that was my choice.

I didn't take out
enough cash at the air-
port ATM, so I had to
choose carefully from
the menu. 20,000 colo-
nes seemed like a lot,
but it was barely worth
$40. I'll find an ATM
tomorrow and see if I
can make myself add
another digit before the
decimal point.

I chose to drink "jugo
naturales   auguas",
which turned out to be
something like a water-

melon slushie and it was delicious! For dinner, I went with the classic arroz con pollo (rice with chicken) and it was SO GOOD!

I really enjoyed the atmosphere in the reggae bar, and you can get just the tiniest sense of it from this photo. Beach front view, great music. Natives and tourists, English and Spanish all mingling together. People smiling, bicycles rolling past, birds and butterflies flitting amongst the rafters. Kinda like paradise...

I've heard that it's possible to sweat out a cold, and if that's true then I should be more than healthy by tomorrow. Here's hoping, since I'm itching to explore!

Day 7 - I'm Melting!
Friday, March 18, 2016

It's so beautiful and green here in Costa Rica, but the unrelenting heat and humidity this close to the equator is far different than my cool northern home of Seattle. The temperature here is a more or less constant mid-80s with thick humidity. The weather report indicates that it gets down to the 70s at night, but it all feels the same to me... sweaty.

In my former life (you know, a week ago) I was very achievement-oriented. I got up early and got stuff done, and just kept going until all of my many responsibilities were completed, then went into vegetation mode for the rest of the day.

But now I no longer have responsibilities, other than to take care of myself and move my body from point A to point B. All I really have to do right now is... BE. That is quite a shift, I'm telling you.

For the first few days of my trip, I was on a schedule and kept up my usual pace. But here, I have nothing scheduled for an entire week. Part of me feels an obligation to get out there and do something, but another part of me recognizes that slowing down to the chilled out (ha!) pace of the Caribbean is exactly what I should be doing right now.

And so I swing in my hammock and enjoy hours of reading novels. I wander down the road to my now favorite place, the reggae bar, for some food and music as I gaze out upon the sea. It took me a couple of days, but I think I'm getting the hang of this whole relaxing thing.

Day 8 - Wildlife and the Wild Life
Saturday, March 19, 2016

The sky was overcast this morning, leading me to finally feel safe in playing in the ocean waves under the open sky. Alas, my sense of security was false, and the rosy glow of my shoulders and back proves it. This close to the equator, even sunblock can't protect skin as fair as mine - espcially still showing a distinct northern pallor.

After frolicking in the sea (and my second cold shower of the day), I wandered about 40 minutes down the one-lane dirt "high-way" along the shore to the Tree of Life Wildlife Sanctuary.

I met my first two-fingered sloths, which are not as common as three-fingered sloths. They'e as cute as I imagined, especially with their plaintive cries of "meh" when hungry or in distress.

The sanctuary is also a botanical garden, which includes the much famed and oh-so-magical theobroma cacao tree (chocolate!) I got to examine the tree from the tiny little bud that will grow into the magnificent cacao pod; from which beans, nibs, and eventually the divine substance of chocolate is derived. I bought a single bar of the homegrown, handmade, organic chocolate manufactured in very small batches from the sanctuary. Oh, such yumminess!

Day 9 - Chillin' in the Heat
Sunday, March 20, 2016

Last night I went back to the reggae bar to enjoy their live Saturday night music. Technically I wasn't at the bar, but across the little dirt road, hanging out on the beach under the moon and enjoying the music without being in the "crowd" of a few dozen people.

I had a marvelous time, swaying to the music (still too hot after dark for actual dancing) and singing along to the many familiar tunes. Even the unfamiliar tunes, like "Death by Coconut" and "Rice and Beans", had catchy melodies and I happily hummed along.

This morning I finally got around to trying the local "pinto" breakfast, which consisted of rice and beans (naturally), along with some tomato, avocado, scrambled eggs, and a couple slices of local cheese. It was delicious and protein-packed, and held me over until dinner time.

I enjoyed a horseback ride in the afternoon. My guide, Raul, asked about my experience level while I got to know my horse. Then we took off down the road while Raul reached out to grab some foliage that works great as a natural insect repellent.

He knew that I had never galloped before and wanted to give me a new experience, so we hit the beach. Aside from the inevitable pounding on my backside as we raced across the black sand at maximum horsepower, the galloping was exhilarating!

Later, I cleaned up and wandered into town for dinner. A sign advertising fresh tuna - my favorite - caught my eye. The thick slab of fish was seared to perfection and served with a refreshing salad and mashed fried plantain cakes, which was all very tasty!

I'm really digging the vibe of this little ocean town. Neither vanity nor modesty seem to exist here. Makeup would be pointless with the constant sheen of sweat on every face. Everyone wears their hair back or up, with sweaty tendrils coming loose.

My uniform has become a tank top and sarong for a skirt. Every once in a while I feel a twinge of modesty as the wind blows open my sarong to expose my thigh up to the hip, but honestly... I've seen a guy wearing a speedo in a restaurant, and plenty of women with their butt cheeks hanging out. Nobody is going to be scandalized by my bare legs!

Day 10 - A Walk en la Parque
Monday, March 21, 2016

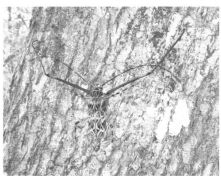

The magnificent insect in this photo is a Harlequin Beetle. The body is 3-4 inches long, and the antennae span 8-9 inches wide. I encountered this mega-bug as I strolled through Cahuita National Park. The park is a roughly 10 km stretch of beachside jungle along the Caribbean coast. There were lots of families camped for the day along the beach – many with large beach umbrellas, and a few even had portable barbecue grills.

The chance to wander in relative comfort through the sun-dappled shade of huge trees and plants was the best part for me. I've learned to stay out of the sun completely in the earlier hours, only coming out to play as the sun begins to wane in the afternoon. I'm still sweating non-stop, but I have much less chance of burning – which has been happening even through my sunblock and SPF 50 parasol.

Another highlight of my park wandering was capturing pictures of a Blue Morpho butterfly, which thoughtfully sat still long enough for me to take a video of it slowly opening and closing its wings to flash that electric blue my way.

I'm now sitting here in the covered outdoor dining area of my cabin while the second impressive tropical rainfall of the day is coming down in full force. The water pressure is intense, and I'm enjoying the cool splashes coming up off the ground.

Day 11 - Final Day in Cahuita
Tuesday, March 22, 2016

On my last day here in Cahuita I was sitting at a bar along the main street of town when I watched one of the many free-roaming dogs get run over by a car right in front of me.

At my horrified gasp, the driver glanced briefly over her shoulder with a look of mild concern and then kept driving. The dog, who seemed more insulted than injured by the incident, rolled over with a yelp and trotted off on four apparently unbroken legs.

Safety standards in Costa Rica are very different than in the USA. I've seen many people riding on motorcycles and scooters, but not one helmet. I've seen pickup trucks with a load of unsecured children having a great time in the back. I've seen a toddler hanging half out of the back window of a moving vehicle, his unconcerned parents in the front. People transport their kids haphazardly in front of them on bikes, scooters, and motorcycles.

I remember being a kid in the 1970s, when seat belts in cars were still something of a novelty to me. These days, it's unthinkable to even drive across a parking lot without being firmly belted in. I remember riding my bike (safely) as a kid without a helmet, which would be against the law where I live now.

I have to wonder... have our extreme standards of safety in the USA really made us safer? Are these parents in Costa Rica actually endangering their children? I don't have answers for those questions... just pondering as I observe the differences in other parts of the world.

Tomorrow I depart this lovely seaside town to move up into the mountains. I'll be trading wifi access for air conditioning, which seems like a pretty fair bargain at this point!

Day 12 - Tree House Hotel (La Fortuna, CR)
Wednesday, March 23, 2016

I arrived at the Tree House Hotel just after sunset. I'm writing this blog sitting on the wraparound porch of my tree house in the jungle in Costa Rica... waiting for a pizza to be delivered by ATV.

Does life get any better? Yes, actually, it does! Because once I go inside, I have air conditioning, a comfy bed, and no bugs waiting to share it.

While my cabin on the beach was amazing and relaxing for the most part, the last couple of nights I spotted ROUSs (roaches of unusual size) scurrying away in the evening. I had to remind myself that they won't actually hurt me, but I was still totally icked out by the knowledge of their presence lurking under my bed.

Day 13 - La Fortuna Waterfall
Thursday, March 24, 2016

I woke to the sounds of the jungle and walked up to the Rancho (outdoor dining area) to enjoy an early morning breakfast before my tour. My host, Lucy, greeted me warmly and offered a cup of tea before serving the fresh breakfast of scrambled eggs with cheese, yucca hash browns, and a wonderful heaping plate of fresh cut tropical fruit.

My adventure today was a horseback ride to La Fortuna Waterfall with my guide, Alberto. After a ride across his private pasture land, crossing a stream, then climbing up a narrow shallow canyon, we dismounted in the horse parking stalls at the top of the falls.

I hiked the 500 steps down to the base of the waterfall on my own. It was still early morning, but there were lots of people already, taking photos and swimming in the river and under the falls. I didn't swim, but waded for a bit before hiking back up those 500 stairs.

After the ride back to Alberto's place, I was welcomed upstairs into their home above the stable, where his daughter-in-law had prepared lunch for me. The homemade chips and homemade salsa were SO yummy, accompanied by fresh tropical juice. The main course was barbecued chicken with a homemade tortilla. More yumminess! I stuffed myself as much as I could before calling a taxi to take me back to the tree house.

A free night hike offered by the hotel rounded out my day. When I mentioned to our guide that I love frogs, he stepped away for a minute and came back with a little toad in his hand. That was only the first of many critters he found for us that night, including the popular red-eyed tree frog and a carnivorous toad.

Day 14 - Arenal Hanging Bridges
Thursday, March 25, 2016

I had another early morning tour booked, and another awesome breakfast at the rancho—coconut waffles with syrup and sweet cream, along with another bountiful plate of fruit. Today's adventure took me to the Arenal Hanging Bridges.

Our guide, Etson, led us into the jungle, keeping a close eye on the foliage to point out any wildlife we encountered. First up was a venomous eyelash viper. We continued on through the jungle, crossing both static and hanging bridges with magnificent vistas as we went.

I was fascinated to learn that trees in the tropics don't grow rings like the trees in northern climates. Since there's no winter and no period of dormancy, trees grow nonstop all year round and never form rings.

As we crossed the final hanging bridge of the tour, I looked up to see a howler monkey in the trees above us. The guide identified her as a female, and then her mate appeared and jumped onto the wires of the bridge above us, howling all the while.

Etson instructed the group to keep our mouths closed – since we were within range to get hit with thrown monkey feces. A couple ahead of our group shouted back that they got hit by the feces already, but my group thankfully escaped without that experience!

After the tour I enjoyed an incredible lunch at a local restaurant. I wandered the tourist shops and listened to a group of musicians before heading back to my tree house. Tired after two days of high activity, I spent the rest of the day lounging and reading.

Day 15 - Arenal Volcano
Saturday, March 26, 2016

At last, a lazy slow morning! Upon waking, I went out to my deck to find that the hotel staff had stealthily delivered my morning tea – a thermos of hot water, along with sugars and cream, to enjoy at my leisure before breakfast. They also set out a banana on the bird feeder attached to my deck so the birds and I could enjoy the morning together.

I sipped my tea while listening to the jungle all around me, then wandered up for breakfast. This morning it was a cheese and potato quiche, two little peanut butter chocolate chip cookies, and my beloved heaping plate of fresh fruit.

Today's plan for a hike on Arenal Volcano was delayed due to a traffic jam. The narrow road was completely blocked by a tow truck, on the scene to pull a vehicle out of the shallow canyon. In typical Costa Rican style, an impromptu street party broke out with all of the vehicles stopped and obviously going nowhere.

Everybody was out of their vehicles and wandering around. Musicians took the opportunity to break out their instruments and entertain the crowd. There were a few vendors selling food on the roadside, so I bought my first ever fresh coconut.

I slaked my thirst draining the liquid out my coconut, then asked my driver if he had a machete (a reasonable question in this part of the world). He did have a very large knife that he used to hack it open, so I spent the rest of the hour-long traffic jam ripping the meat out of the fresh coconut with my fingers and loving every bite of it.

We topped off the day with a stop at Paradise Hot Springs at the base of the volacano. It was a gorgeous evening to float languidly in the geo-thermally heated water after hours of mountain hiking.

I cannot recommend the Tree Houses Hotel highly enough. The hosts, Mark and Lucy, treat every guest like family. They know every guest's name and preferences. They provide 5-star service in the heart of the Costa Rican jungle, arranging tours with the best and most trustworthy guides, and serving incredible breakfasts every day. I don't want to leave, but there are more experiences to be had!

Day 17 - Pura Vida (San Jose, Costa Rica)
Monday, March 28, 2016

There's a phrase often repeated here in Costa Rica – pura vida. Literally translated, it means "pure life". In common usage, it's a greeting and farewell, as well as thank you and pretty much anything else. It's a philosophy and a way of life, recognizing the inherent easy-going goodness in being alive. And it's my new personal motto!

Last night after I arrived at my hostel, I found the inner courtyard where many of the guests hangout. I sat down with my laptop at a large table with one other woman and we struck up a conversation with the standard greeting among travelers – "where are you from?"

I found that she's from Memphis and traveling without a plan for the first time ever – letting her destinations be determined by faith and her spirit guides. She asked if she could give me a tarot reading, saying that her guides had some messages for me.

I agreed and we had such a great connection chatting that we decided to spend some more time together the next day, taking a long stroll in the nearby park. We spoke of faith and trust, family, life, love, and more. We each gave each other many gifts of insight through our discussion, and it was an altogether amazing time.

And then there was a misunderstanding. I have many healers and mystics among my friends and I'm accustomed to sharing our gifts freely. The thought to offer cash for her tarot reading hadn't occured to me.

When she later approached me for a heart to heart conversation explaining my insult to her, and requesting that I pay her hundreds of dollars, I was blindsided. We each shared our thoughts and feelings on the matter, but neither of us felt good about the outcome.

There are lessons to be found in all interactions and I'm sure I'll learn from this as well. Communication is so important to me and I feel some sense of failure in this misunderstanding.

Thinking back on the concept of pura vida, our brief friendship was such a great example of the easy-going flow of loving life. However, there is also a natural balance in all things. A full life is not only goodness, but often pain and hardship as well.

I suppose the lesson is taking it all in stride, and no matter what, facing each new day with the expectation of more goodness coming my way than anything else. Pura vida!

Day 19 - Waking up in Ollantaytambo, Peru
Wedenesday, March 30, 2016

It was a long journey from Costa Rica through one night in a Lima airport hotel and another day of short (though delayed) flights to

Cusco, followed by a two-hour cab ride. My sister Jennifer and I finally arrived in the Incan village of Ollantaytambo after dark.

The night sky is amazing here, and I was delighted to bask in the glow of countless stars, with even the Milky Way is visible. We were warmly welcomed to our accommodation, Casa de Wow, and offered our choice of rooms - all with rustic beds handmade by Wow, himself.

We were both feeling the effects of the high altitude at 9,160 feet, so we sat down in the kitchen to enjoy our first cups of coca tea with mint and honey. (Raw coca leaves come from the same plant that produces cocaine after a lot of processing.)

While we enjoyed our delicious and stimulating tea, our host told us about some tours of the Sacred Valley. We decided that tomorrow we'll take a half-day horseback ride up a nearby mountain and through some Incan ruins.

I was exhausted from three nights of interrupted sleep and went to bed shortly after we finished our tea. The climate here is much cooler than the tropics of Costa Rica, but we were both comfortable leaving the window open to enjoy the cool night air.

I awoke this morning to the sound of a wooden cart being pulled up the rough cobblestone street two stories below. The view of

Incan ruins from our window promises some great photo opportunities!

Day 20 - Cave of Bones
Thursday, March 31, 2016

There were two horses waiting for us outside the casa in the morning and I was immediately drawn to the curly-haired mare. We mounted up and our guide, Mario, led us out of town, across the river, and on our way up one of the many mountains that border the Sacred Valley.

We encountered several large, brilliant-green hummingbirds darting among the flowers along the way. Continuing upwards on the narrow rocky trail, the mountainside dropped away sharply only inches from the hooves of our horses. There were a few times when we had to hug the mountain side to make room for locals with pack horses and other groups of tourists passing us in the opposite direction.

After a two-hour ride up to a grassy plain, we dismounted to give our panting horses a rest. Although our guide spoke only Spanish, we understood when he indicated that there was more to see if we continued up hiking on foot.

He pointed out several column-like stones that were remnants of Incan settlements, and the huge boulders nearby from which those large stones had been cut. He then pointed out an opening in the rock, which is where we found the cave of bones.

I recognized the site as a sacred place, and so prepared to offer a gift of one of the small stones that I bring with me for such occasions. When I opened my pouch, an unpolished garnet jumped out and I knew that the right offering had made itself known. I paused to ask silently for permission before ducking my head to enter the tiny cave.

There were human skulls, spinal columns, femurs, a rib cage, and other bones visible at the cave entrance and farther back on stone ledges. There was a fresh green apple sitting on a shelf, which is where I also placed my garnet. Paying my respects to the spirits of the place, I backed out of the small space.

We hiked up a bit more and were shown a large stone wheel, also a remnant from the Incans. The tour was fascinating, but we were both feeling the effects of altitude on top of altitude and it was time to go.

I had purchased some coca-candy to help us cope with the altitude, but the stimulating sweets were no match for our headaches, shaking legs, and light headedness. By the time we got back to the casa, we were both totally exhausted and dehydrated.

We each chugged a couple bottles of water, then Jennifer rested while I went out in search of food. I enjoyed a fruit smoothie and an alpaca steak (much like carne asada) before surrendering to my own exhaustion. It's now 6:30pm and I'm ready for bed, even as I sit here drinking another cup of coca tea.

Tomorrow may be a good day to rest!

Day 21 - Shopping in Ollantaytambo
Friday, April 01, 2016

After a solid eleven hours of sleep, Jennifer and I both woke up feeling much restored this morning, even if still a bit sore from the long horseback ride yesterday. We enjoyed a slow and easy morning, with another breakfast of coca tea, scrambled eggs, and fresh rolls.

Then we strolled into town to find a cash machine and made our way to the morning market where most of the locals shop. The market was a three-story building with open walkways looking down on the lower floors. Vendors were set up in small stalls and along the walls.

The first floor was mostly produce and meat products. There were many fruits and vegetables that we didn't recognize, and oddly shaped versions of familiar items like very short, very wide carrots, and strangely lumpy potatoes.

I felt like walking through a house of horrors when we got to the meat department. First I noticed the whole plucked chickens (heads and feet still intact). Next came the disembodied head of a cow, followed by whole skinless goats and sheep hanging from hooks with blood dripping onto the white tile floor below. There was a bloody axe stuck in a wooden stump next to the hanging carcasses. No tidy wrapped packages of meat here!

Next we made our way to the second floor, which had vendors offering prepared foods; and non-food items like comic books, clothes, bags, and electronic goods. We enjoyed some really great juice smoothies from one of the second floor vendors.

By now we've learned to pace ourselves in this high altitude climate, so we went back to the casa to rest for a bit before continuing our explorations. Later we wandered down the road to the street vendors by the train station. A very friendly older Peruvian lady helped Jennifer find a gorgeous alpaca wool sweater, then kissed both of us on the cheeks in parting.

Upon entering a shop advertising jewelry, I was drawn to a row of drums. I found one with lovely tone and the price was right. I'm now the proud owner of a cactus-base, goatskin-head drum, which is being shipped back to the States for me!

We were feeling tired and drained again, but the Chocolate Museum was conveniently just a few doors up from where we were, featuring an outdoor café with shaded area for lounging. We each ordered an iced chocolate beverage (which was awesome) and shared some potato chips with guacamole to refresh ourselves.

We have one more full day to explore Ollantaytambo tomorrow, and I'm hoping we'll find the energy (and breath, with the thin oxygen here) to climb up to some of the ruins. Until tomorrow, mis amigos!

Day 22 - Getting High
Saturday, April 02, 2016

On our final day in Ollantaytambo, it was time to check out some of the amazing archeological sites here. First up was the National Archeological Park in town, which involved another climb up about 1,500 more feet - as if the altitude in town wasn't enough!

We enjoyed the incredible views of the Sacred Valley afforded by the additional height, and got an up-close look at the Incan architecture. The walls of this site are constructed in the same fashion of Machu Picchu – no mortar, just huge stones shaped to fit with such exact precision that no mortar is needed. Even the corners were beautifully fit and rounded.

After a quick stop for a repeat of the same iced chocolate drink that we enjoyed yesterday, we were beckoned by a cab driver who made a fair offer to take us exactly where we wanted to go next.

Less than an hour away, we arrived at Moras Moray (11,500 feet elevation), another Incan ruin with terraced concentric circles carved deep into the hillside. There's little known about the original purpose of the site, but it resembles a large amphitheater, and historians have suggested it may have been used to test agriculture at various elevations.

Exhausted once more from altitude and hiking, we returned to Casa de Wow for our final night. We did our best to take the day's activities slow and easy, but we both still feel unusually wiped out far earlier in the day than we expected. That's the effect of altitude on sea-level dwellers like we Seattle-ites!

Day 23 – Stormy
Sunday, April 03, 2016

I woke this morning feeling almost more tired than when I went to bed last night. I loved our accommodation for the first few nights, but then more guests arrived and it began to get very crowded.

As I sat at the small kitchen table last night writing my blog, the room became very crowded with other guests preparing meals and gathering to socialize. I'm an introvert with a greater than average need for personal space, so that was making me very uncomfortable.

The beautiful timber floors of the casa become very loud and bouncy with lots of people walking over them, and the shared bathroom became wet, dirty, and without toilet paper in a hurry due to the full house. My sleep was disturbed in the wee hours by a child crying, a cell phone ringing, and the floor (along with my bed) bouncing each time someone used the bathroom next to our room.

So my day started a bit cranky, but then we enjoyed first class service in the Vistadome train from Ollantaytambo to the town at the base of Machu Picchu, Aguas Calientes. The views were amazing, and the service was great for the 90 minute ride.

We arrived and negotiated the labyrinth of vendor booths to find our way out of the train station. Using one of the three bridges in town, we crossed the river and walked the short distance to our B&B alongside the Rio Aguas Calientes.

We set out to explore the small town after taking a few minutes to freshen up in our room. When we'd gotten just about as far away from the B&B as we could get without leaving town, rain started dripping and then gushing from the sky. Taking shelter from the storm, we stepped into one of the many restaurants along the main street offering a four-course fixed price dinner menu.

We each enjoyed a different avocado-based appetizer, followed by a soup course. Next came grilled chicken for Jennifer, and grilled trout (a local specialty) for me. Dessert was crepes with chocolate sauce. Fortunately, the portion sizes were small enough that we could enjoy the whole meal without stuffing ourselves, and the food was great!

Our table featured a game of Jenga, which we played while waiting for our meal. Many of the wooden blocks were inscribed with names, dates, and artwork from fellow travelers who had left their mark, and so we inscribed our own block after dinner.

Later we met our guide for orientation to our Machu Picchu tour in the morning, but we had difficulty understanding his English. We're both very excited for the tour tomorrow, and it's unlikely that either of us will ever return to Peru given its distance from our homes, so we were distraught at the thought of not being able to clearly understand and learn from our guide. I brought our concerns to the B&B receptionist who booked the tour for us and he quickly arranged for another guide.

So we're both still a little tired and cranky, but holding high hopes for a great day with an early morning start tomorrow.

Day 24 - Machu Picchu
Monday, April 04, 2016

25 minutes of zigzagging up narrow mountain switchbacks with breathtaking cliffs overlooking the valley below led us to the gated entrance to the city of Machu Picchu. We connected with our guide, who spoke excellent English as promised.

Our guide, Hamilton, rallied our group of twelve people and led us through the entrance gate. Our first glimpse of mountain views and Incan ruins was nothing less than awe inspiring! The day was brightly sunny with plenty of fluffy white clouds in the deep blue sky for contrast, and the green grass of the many terraces added to the spectacle of color and grandiose natural beauty.

We sat on the edge of one of the terraces (with llamas roaming freely) while Hamilton went over some of the history and speculation about Machu Picchu. It was discovered by an American archeologist in 1911, and opened for tourism in 1948, but was built and occupied by its original inhabitants in the 14th century.

The tour continued for two and a half hours through the ruined city, with highlights like the Incan compass (mirroring the stars) and the sun dial. Another highlight was the reflecting pools, for gazing indirectly at the sun and moon, which were sacred to these people.

We also learned that, in this large city meant to house about 700 people, there was only one toilet and it was reserved for the king alone. (It's good to be the king!)

When the tour was completed, Jennifer and I went our separate ways for a couple of hours. She hiked up to the Incan bridge, and I wandered Machu Picchu to find a quiet place for solitude and reflection.

I found a perfect spot with a little stone bench and overhanging rock that provided protection from the occasional sprinkles of rain, with an amazing view of the surrounding Andes Mountains.

As I was settling into the vibe of the place, a bird landed near

me and started hopping even closer. The little bird had no fear and came up only inches from my feet, looking me straight in the eye. I took that as my official welcome to Machu Picchu. When more tourists walked by, my feathered friend flew away.

We're looking forward to a slow and lazy day tomorrow, sleeping late before visiting the hot springs after which the town of Aguas Calientes is named.

Day 26 – Body
Wednesday, April 06, 2016

Please enjoy this photo of mystic mountain mama llama, which I took at Machu Picchu the other day and is totally unrelated to this blog post. I was sick yesterday, and barely had enough energy to open my eyes, let alone get out for photo-worthy adventures!

After several long days of hiking, exploring, and adventuring, I started to get that gurgley belly feeling in the evening. By morning I was in full blown gastric distress, followed by such a dra-

58

matic drop in my energy that I literally spent the entire day in bed. I just pushed myself too far and my body went on strike.

Fortunately, my sister was here and took good care of me – checking on me every couple of hours and making sure that I got whatever food and drink I could take.

By evening, I felt well enough to go out into town for dinner. The meal recovered some of my severely depleted energy, then I went back to bed for a nice long night's sleep. By this morning I was back to my usual healthy self.

I would just like to say for the record how much I LOVE MY BODY. I've asked a lot of my body over the last four weeks – dealing with uncomfortable climates, new foods, questionable water, interrupted sleep, and far more exercise than usual. I've suffered minor sunburns, bug bites, bumps and bruises. And for the most part, my body has taken it all in stride with little complaint.

My American sensibilities tell me that if my body isn't perfectly proportioned, gloriously tan and toned, and ready for a Playboy centerfold from every angle... that it can't be a good body.

But the fact of the matter is, my body is a tool that allows me to travel all over this amazing planet and it functions exceptionally well. I have an awesome body! I am loving my body more each day for what it allows me to experience of this world, regardless of what society has conditioned me to believe about myself.

Since I'm feeling better today, we went ahead with our lazy slow day plan for yesterday. After breakfast, we wandered up to the highest point in town - the hot springs from which Aguas Calientes gets its name. The springs are well-maintained tiled pools, some with smooth bottoms and some with loose gravel.

There were few other visitors to the springs so early in the day, and we enjoyed a nice long soak in relative solitude. Just as I was hoping, the weather kicked in and we got to enjoy a cool rainstorm from the comfort of the hot springs.

The rain continued on, so we shared a lemonade in the lounge while trying to wait out the storm. The lounge featured several comfy seating areas with plentiful works of art and open-air views of the lush plant life and surrounding mountain vistas.

Most of the art centered around the theme of the three spiritual realms recognized by the indigenous people of the Andes Mountains: the lower realm represented by Snake, the middle realm represented by Puma, and the upper realms by Condor.

We ended up walking back to the B&B in the rain, then later went out to peruse the many vendor booths on the train station side of town. I found a gorgeous silver cuff bracelet featuring spirals, which is the symbol of the Pachamama, or Earth mother goddess.

While I don't consider myself a good negotiator, I only had $50 cash on me, and so the vendor accepted what I had rather than the $68 she was asking for the bracelet. I call that a successful day!

Day 27 - Reflections on Peru
Thursday, April 07, 2016

On my final day I'd like to share some of my observations on Peru.

SEXY LLAMAS: On my first day in Ollantaytambo, I saw the sign for a place called the Sexy Llama Bar. I thought that was just one person's cute idea and it made me giggle, but then I heard the phrase repeated too many times in different locations for it to be coincidence. Sexy llamas were even mentioned by our guide at Machu Picchu.

I don't know. Standards of beauty are unique to each culture, so maybe the elegance of their four long legs or the flirtatious twitch of their furry tails is the epitome of sexy? That will have to remain a mystery for another trip.

BATHROOMS: I'm happy enough to have found seats on most of the toilets I encountered, but used paper isn't flushed in the toilets of Peru. Instead, there's a little trash bin next to the commode to collect soiled paper. That receptacle can get a little ripe, especially when sharing a bathroom that isn't maintained several times daily.

PEOPLE: The residents of the Andes Mountains in Peru are amazingly tough. While my sister and I huffed and puffed with the slightest exertion in this high-altitude low-oxygen atmosphere, the natives are carrying huge heavy packs over the multi-day hikes of the Incan trail and running at the end of it! It might take an average person 60-90 minutes to hike to one of the highest peaks around Machu Picchu, but the fastest record for a native was around twelve minutes.

Not only are they physically strong and fast (and compact, with the average height of the people a few inches over five feet), but they have achieved incredible feats of architecture and engineering. Machu Picchu is an unimaginable construction high in the mountain peaks. The native village of Ollantaytambo has blended with modern technology to become a fully functioning modern city with omnipresent wifi even in this remote location (although the plumbing still needs work.)

The vendors and restaurant workers are what I call aggressively friendly, especially in Aguas Calientes. We couldn't walk ten feet down the street without several people calling out to us, showing us their menus, offering free drinks, asking our names and home towns.

Walking through a row of vendors involves almost every single one of them showing off their wares, even though they're all selling exactly the same merchandise. (Seriously... hundreds of vendors, and the same alpaca wool sweaters, the same leather wallets stamped with "Cusco", and the same fluffy llama toys in every stall.)

Nonetheless, we visited almost every vendor and were introduced to at least half of them. Everywhere we went in Peru felt safe and welcoming. The land is awe inspiring and its people warm and sincere.

Day 28 - Intermediate Level (Sao Paulo, Brazil)
Friday, April 08, 2016

My first four weeks of travel were all in Spanish-speaking destinations and I got pretty comfortable communicating with my very limited vocabulary, but this morning I arrived in Brazil, where Portuguese is spoken. And while the two languages share a lot of similarities, there are enough differences that I'm feeling totally out of my element again.

I arrived tired, but on time to Sao Paulo airport after my crowded overnight flight. I'm happy that I had the foresight to pre-arrange private transportation to my hotel, because I was in no condition to strategize public transportation at that point.

The taxi service was excellent, texting to let me know when my driver arrived to pick me up. Sergio spoke English very well and helped me learn some important words in Portuguese over the two-hour drive (since I kept speaking Spanish in my sleep deprived state.)

We arrived at my hotel around 8am, where I paid for an extra half day to check in early so that I could get some sleep immediately. And after a two-hour nap I was ready for some exploring.

I hadn't eaten much over the last 24 hours of travel and my body needed fuel, so I went in search of food. I stuck my head into one restaurant, but didn't immediately see a menu and didn't know the right word to ask for one. The waitress and I tried unsuccessfully to communicate for a minute or so, then I just smiled, thanked her and went on my way.

Hot, sweaty, and increasingly hungry, I wandered on until I found a place that appeared to offer casual sandwiches.

I had a bit more success communicating at this place by using my limited Spanish. I managed to ask for a menu and chose one of the few items I could recognize – a salami sandwich. It was delightful, and I enjoyed it with an ice cold glass bottle of Coke. I even managed cash payment at the end of my meal with relative ease, and so I returned to my hotel feeling very accomplished.

(It's the little things!)

I've spent most of this day in the air conditioned comfort of my room, posting reviews and going over photos. Not wanting to repeat my lunch confusion, I reseached nearby restaurants for some indication of English spoken. I also spent quite a bit of time translating online menus so that I could determine what I want to eat for dinner and how to properly communicate my order. (Yay for google translate!)

But as fate would have it... the restaurant I so carefully prepared for was closed for business. Instead, I found an ice cream shop and managed with gestures and smiles to ask for what I wanted. Then I found a mini market for some bread, cheese, and bottled water to tide me over until tomorrow.

From the beginning of my trip planning, I've felt a distinct shift at this point in my itinerary. The relative familiarity of the Americas will soon be behind me and I'll be muddling through new languages at least once a week.

The best I can hope is to learn how to be polite in each language (hello, please, thank you), but the time has now come to simply embrace the unknown and trust in the kindness of strangers to help me through it.

I'm fiercely independent, and allowing myself to need help from others is deeply challenging for me. The last thing I want is to appear as an "ignorant American" – insisting that everyone around me cater to my English without even bothering to attempt the local language.

It would have been great if I had taken the time and effort to become fluent in Spanish, Portuguese, Italian, Greek, Keralam, Bahasa Malaysia, and Balinese... but that is nowhere near realistic. And so I'll just have to cut myself some slack, do my best, and stumble through the language barriers with a smile and as much grace as I can manage.

I've completed my beginning level of travel with my first month through the Americas, and now I'm on to the wide variety of countries and cultures I'll encounter for the next two and a half months. Time to really hone those communication skills I've been practicing all along!

Day 29 - Missions Accomplished
Saturday, April 09, 2016

I spent most of today in my air conditioned room, catching up on business with high speed internet. It was hot and sweaty out there again and I just wasn't motivated to go out in the heat, but I still had a few goals for the day that required leaving the hotel.

First, I still had a sushi craving after finding the restaurant I researched yesterday closed. I chose a nearby place where a member of their kitchen staff was learning English. She was happy for the chance to practice with me, so there were no communication problems. First mission accomplished!

My second mission, to find hair gel, was far more challenging than I expected. I tried a grocery store, but they only had one option and I didn't like the smell of it. Next I tried a drug store and couldn't find any hair styling products at all. Then I wandered past the window of a fancy salon shop, but couldn't see anything past the outrageous prices.

Finally I wandered into another drug store and someone immediately asked if they could help me. By now, I've taught myself how to say that I don't speak Portuguese, and the lady eagerly went to get someone who could understand my question.

A male employee came over and took my hand, asking how he could help. (I don't know if I looked like I needed emotional support, or if hand-holding customers is just a thing in Brazil.) He helped me find a lightly scented hair cream that should work with my curls, and that mission was accomplished as well.

And last but never least, I wanted more ice cream! I wasn't sure of the protocol when I went to an ice cream shop last night, but tonight I found a shop with a long line and it became obvious that this is a scoop-your-own culture.

There were a couple of dozen options in freezer cases, with several scoopers in water in front of the cases. I scooped out some chocolate, lemon, and a red fruity flavor. They weighed my selections and tried to ask me questions at the register, but "nao falo Portuguese" and a smile was all the answer I could give. Nonetheless, the price was displayed on the register, so I paid for my purchase and left to enjoy my treat while walking back towards the beach.

With the sun down, the beach vendors with drinks, umbrellas, and chairs were packing up for the day. However, there were still hundreds of people playing in the waves, walking, jogging, and playing all over the beach. I walked barefoot among the incoming waves while looking for a quieter spot to perform a little ritual.

Tomorrow I depart on my 14-night cruise, so I wanted to make an offering to the ocean for safe passage. I took a minute to ground and center myself while letting three waves wash over my feet. I called silently to each of the four directions for their blessings, then threw one of my special stones as far as I could out into the water. May the passage be safe and successful.

Now I can relax in my room for the rest of the evening, enjoying the mini bottle of Jameson whiskey I bought from duty-free with my last few Peruvian soles at the airport, and fast enough internet to kick back with a little Netflix!

Day 31 - On Board (Transatlantic Cruise)
Monday, April 11, 2016

Processing through checked baggage, health screening, and identification verification at the cruise terminal in Santos went smoothly... although every single person I came in contact with seemed a little confused and concerned by my solo status. However, I did see other travelers who appeared to be alone.

Once on board, I dropped off my small bag in my stateroom, then went off to enjoy the lunch buffet and explore the ship. I naturally gravitated toward the spa, where I was sucked in by the "discount" sales pitch to buy three services at increasing percentages off.

The woman giving me the spa tour happened to be a manicurist from the Philippines and she suggested that I try her services right away. My hands and feet have taken a lot of abuse over the last month of travel, so I agreed.

Annabelle started with my manicure, paying special attention to massaging my hands and arms. Next came the pedicure, in a fancy massage chair overlooking the harbor. We spoke of our lives and families off the ship while she worked on me.

When I was done at the spa it was time for the muster drill (standard safety procedure for cruising.) Every passenger was required to be out on deck while crew members shouted instructions in several different languages and tried to control the passengers who were all eager to get back to the buffet.

After the muster drill and a quick shower, it was time for dinner in the main dining room, where I met some of my dinner companions for the duration of the trip. There were two couples from Malta - longtime travel companions, each celebrating 40+ years of marriage - and we had a great time getting to know each other.

My dinner companions planned to see the live show after we ate, but I was more interested in the poolside screening of "Interstellar", so we went our separate ways.

The ship was well underway and listing side to side, causing the swimming pool to slosh huge amounts of water over both sides with the movement of the boat. The wind was also pretty extreme up on deck nine where the movie was showing.

I retired to my stateroom after the movie. I didn't realize how much the ship vibrated until I laid down, and experienced the cruise version of "magic fingers" through my mattress. It took me a little longer than usual to fall asleep with the intermittent vibrations, but eventually the motion of the ocean lulled me into peaceful slumber.

Day 32 - Rio de Janeiro
Tuesday, April 12, 2016

On Monday morning the ship docked in Rio de Janeiro. I had booked an excursion to visit the rainforest, but it was cancelled due to lack of interest. (Perhaps due to fear of zika virus.) Other tours offered to the iconic Christ the Redeemer statue and trips to Ipanema or Copacabana beaches didn't appeal to me so I decided to go it alone and see what the city had to offer on foot (humming Copacabana all the while.)

After stuffing myself silly at the breakfast buffet (seriously, it was embarrassing, but what else can you do when faced with an unlimited supply of bacon?), I grabbed my parasol and headed off the ship to see what I could see. Although its autumn here in the southern hemisphere, Brazil hasn't gotten that memo yet. The day was brilliantly sunny and near 90 degrees, not to mention humid.

The cruise terminal was under heavy construction in preparation for the Olympic Games to be hosted in this city in the near future. Once I figured out how to get out (past a slew of aggressive cab drivers who all believed I needed a ride), I chose a direction and started to wander.

The city has thoughtfully installed tourist maps, as well as many directional signs pointing the way (and estimated time to walk) to destinations of interest – including the cruise terminal. The signs indicated a Museum of Art and a Museum of Tomorrow in the same direction, so that's the way I wandered.

I came upon a plaza with the word-art shown below. It's a beautiful installation that changes appearance as you move around it. From the front the letters are white, but as you move around it, you can see that each letter is covered in colorful art.

As it turns out, museums in Rio are closed on Mondays so I didn't get to visit those. I was already feeling sweaty and overheated from my walk, so I just headed back to the ship, chugged a couple of glasses of water, then enjoyed a small salad for first lunch.

Later I returned to the buffet for second lunch (like any good Hobbit.) I began feeling like this buffet thing could get out of hand quickly, so I decided to limit myself to dessert only twice each day. (Note: I didn't say only two desserts, I said only twice. I ended up having two desserts with lunch and three with dinner.)

In the main dining room at dinner time, the two Maltese couples were there again at our table, along with three Americans who hadn't joined us the first night. They were all experienced cruisers and taught me that ordering multiple appetizers, entrees, and desserts is expected. Considering that the portion of calamari I ordered was only three rings, I started to understand the all-inclusive dining system.

I went back to my room to relax before going out to enjoy one of the evening shows, but the gentle rocking of the ship in motion made me sleepy and I chose to stay "home" reading my book and called it an early night.

Day 34 - Battle of the Bed
Wednesday, April 13, 2016

While my 'panoramic view' stateroom is lovely and comfortable for the most part, the bed seems to have turned against me. The first night I slept OK. The second night I was tossing and turning, and had unpleasant dreams. By the end of the second day, my back was twinging and threatening to spasm.

In the first 30 days of sleeping in a wide variety of beds – including one mildly sketchy hostel – my body never complained about the beds. But two nights in this one and my back just wasn't having it.

By dinner time last night, I had a little shooting pain in my low back each time I leaned forward. I decided to take a dip in the hot tub later on in the hope of soothing my irritated muscles. Watching the nightly poolside movie from the hot tub with a fat crescent moon shining in the sky above was just a bonus!

When I returned to my room, I really didn't want to find out what a third night in that bed would do to me, so I took the cushions from my couch, the pillows and blankets from the bed, and made myself comfortable on the floor for the night. I still tossed and turned with oddly disturbing dreams, but at least I woke with less pain!

Since Royal Caribbean keeps touting their "we'll do anything to make you more happy and comfortable" attitude, I decided to let them put my mattress where their mouth is, so to speak.

I went to guest services and explained the situation (including that I had slept on the floor), asking if a firmer mattress was available. They said yes, right away, and so I went off on my excursion in Salvador de Bahia looking forward to a more comfortable rest tonight.

When I booked the tour I didn't understand that it was nothing more than hours of riding around in an air conditioned bus listening to a guide alternate between English and Portuguese. I did learn a few things, but I had really been looking forward to a chance to walk and exercise my aching back – not more time seated! Ah, well.

I returned to the ship and walked into my stateroom hoping for the best. The bed was still noticeably concave in the middle – not a good sign. I went to guest services again to see when I should expect the mattress exchange. After a few calls they discovered the problem. My mattress had already been exchanged for one that's softer! (Oy vey.)

Not only did they misunderstand my request, but then I was told that my original mattress is the firmest that they have. (Seriously? I can't be the only person in the world who needs something a bit more supportive than ultra-squishy.)

I'm prepared to sleep on the floor again tonight if I have to, but this time I'll leave my makeshift pallet for my stateroom attendant to find in the morning. Perhaps I can enlist his help in finding a mattress that will allow me a good night's sleep without pain…

Day 35 - Sea Dreams and Seaweed
Thursday, April 14, 2016

I'm pleased to report that the Battle of the Bed was resolved peacefully with a brand new extra-firm mattress, and my back is once again happy. However, the odd and mildly disturbing dreams continue.

I suspect that the constant rocking and rolling motion of the ocean waves that makes me feel so sleepy during the day is also preventing me from entering deep sleep for very long at night. I wake up several times in the night, frequently drifting in and out of REM sleep and experience far more dreams.

The first four days of the cruise followed the Brazilian coast northward with two ports of call, but last night we began the eastward journey into the open ocean for the next six days.

Today I enjoyed the second of the three spa treatments that I booked in advance – a seaweed wrap. The technician brought me to what I can only describe as a wet massage room, complete with shower. I was instructed to disrobe and put on the disposable underwear that she provided, then lay face down on the massage table, which was covered in several large sheets of thin metallic material.

The technician returned to the room and laid a large towel over me, then began using a stiff-bristled brush to exfoliate my whole body from my toes upward. Application of the warm seaweed mud all over the back of my body was next. Then she asked me to flip over, providing a small towel to drape over my breasts before slathering the seaweed over the front of my body (including my belly, which is a very odd sensation if you're not used to that area being touched!)

Once I was basted in seaweed mud, she wrapped the aluminum foil sheets completely around me and added a towel on top to keep me warm. Thankfully, my head wasn't covered in the body-burrito, so she gave me a lovely scalp and face massage while the seaweed and aluminum wrap worked its magic.

The timer went off and I was helped into a seated position while she removed the wrappings. Then she directed me into the shower to wash off the mud. I was happy enough to be able to do that part myself (now totally naked, of course), but when I tried to get out of the shower she pointed me back to it, and scrubbed the remaining mud off those posterior regions that I couldn't see.

Then it was back onto the table with more wrapping, this time for an extensive foot massage while the rest of me cooked in the foil. Then back into the shower, but thankfully I didn't appear to need help that time. I returned to the table for a third time, for a more classical massage to finish up the treatment.

When I booked the spa treatments, an automatic 18% gratuity was added to the cost. I thought that was fair, and was then surprised to be asked if I wanted to offer an additional gratuity. Awkward! What's the etiquette for voluntary tipping on top of mandatory tipping, especially when someone has just washed your naked backside for you?

And of course, this question of additional tipping came up after she offered me an array of expensive spa products to help with my "problem areas", and I declined. Although the ship is definitely service-oriented, it feels like all of the friendly and gracious service tends to come with additional expectations to buy more and spend more. As a naturally frugal person on a tight budget, that is disconcerting, especially when I don't want to offend the people providing me with service.

I asked the technician if she would receive the 18% auto-gratuity and she said that she would. Then I asked about the etiquette of tipping on top of it, and her response was a non-committal, "you can tip more if you want to." I added another $5 and hoped that wasn't offensive.

Before I left my room for the massage, I had left a note of thanks along with $20 for my stateroom attendant, with gratitude for all of the mattress switching yesterday (including freshly making each new bed.) I wanted him to know that his extra efforts are appreciated – even though I've already paid the required auto-gratuity for housekeeping in advance as well.

I'm not an ungenerous person, but I don't like to feel pressure to continually give more than I expect to pay. However, I'm afraid that may just be part of the whole cruise experience. We're all here on this boat to spend, spend, and spend some more. I should probably just surrender to it, but it kinda goes against my nature.

Day 36 - Land Ho!
Friday, April 15, 2016

On our second full day at sea, I was awoken early in the morning by an announcement from the captain. We were passing the Fernando de Noronha Archipelago (a World Heritage Site and municipality of Brazil), which is the last land we'll see until the Canary Islands next week.

After about 48 hours of nothing but open ocean, that was exciting enough for me to jump out of bed, throw on some clothes, and run up to an upper deck to see. (Life can get a little dull on these multiple sea days.) That excitement passed quickly since we didn't actually stop at any of those islands.

With nothing pressing on the agenda, I went back to bed to read for a while before breakfast. This morning I chose a table overlooking the bow of the ship, where I could watch a dozen black and white seagulls playing games with the air currents

around the boat. These gulls are different from the plumper (french fry loving) gray seagulls of Seattle who frequent the area around Ivar's waterfront restaurant.

The seagulls were pretty much the highlight of my day. I later went out to another deck to lounge in one of the many chairs with my feet up on the rail and watch the birds. The day's entertainment was rounded out by a showing of Star Wars: The Force Awakens in the on-board theater, followed by dinner in the main dining room again.

Upon hearing the dulcet strains of "YCMA" from the center atrium just now, I ran out to watch other guests performing the traditional dance of The Village People. (I think I may be starving for quality entertainment out here.) Later tonight we officially cross the equator and tomorrow there will be a ceremony in celebration. Here's hoping for a bit more excitement to report after that!

Day 37 – Imperium Neptuni Regis
Saturday, April 16, 2016

When my paternal grandfather ("Pop", to all who knew him) was in the US Navy as a young man, he crossed the equator on a ship and was given a beautiful certificate featuring King Neptune, mermaids, and other fantastic creatures of the sea to commemorate the occasion.

I was fascinated that the US military (steeped in stifling stuffiness, from my perspective) would create such a fanciful memento. I had such a fondness for my grandfather's certificate that I took great care in restoring it and preserving it with museum-quality matting and frame. It now hangs in my father's office at home.

It was my grandfather's experience in crossing the equator that inspired me to take this cruise. Although I'll cross the equator a total of four times by the end of my journey, it was important to me to cross once on the planet's surface. I was utterly delighted to return to my stateroom tonight to find my very own equatorial-crossing memento!

Mine isn't as elaborate or pretty as Grandpa Pop's, but he worked for his and I'm just playing my way through Neptune's realm.

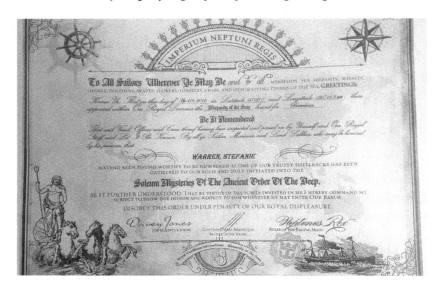

The actual crossing occurred last night around 9:30pm. There were many more people than usual out on the top deck. (I've been moon gazing in the evenings, and there isn't usually anybody else outside at that time.) Nobody could miss it when the Captain let forth with three very long, very loud blasts of the ship's horn to announce our crossing.

Everyone ran to the rails to peer out into the water, but the equator looks exactly like the rest of the ocean. No buoys, no lights, no dotted line on the water. A little anti-climactic, but satisfying to me anyway.

The ship's crew put on an official ceremony (more of a pageant, really) by the pool this afternoon. A fake-bearded Neptune and his vaguely Roman attendants paraded down the stairs and onto the pool deck to the sea-themed throne that had been prepared for him. They were followed by a queen in a mermaid-esque green sequined gown with toga-clad attendants of her own.

Altogether, it was kinda cute, and definitely cheesy. I just hope that we honored Neptune sufficiently without offering insult to the Ruler of the Raging Main.

Day 38 - The Middle of Nowhere
Sunday, April 17, 2016

Well, here we are. Bobbing on top of a vast blue ocean… far, far away from ANYthing as the Captain reminded us earlier today, describing our navigational position as "the middle of nowhere."

I'm deeply grateful to the King County Library system, which has kept me well supplied with e-books to entertain myself during this long journey. Although the ship puts out a full list of activities every day, the vast majority of them are either silly poolside games (too much sunshine) or thinly veiled attempts to sell more stuff. (Hint: a makeover isn't "free" if you have to purchase $150 in product to get it.)

However, I was very happy to find an event on the schedule today that actually caught my interest – an invitation to form a ship's choir! I joined a group of people gathering around a grand piano in the central atrium. There were about a dozen of us, evenly split between Portuguese speakers and English speakers, plus one lone Spanish speaker.

With two facilitators and three languages, our newly formed choir had the task of agreeing on four songs to learn and present to the rest of the ship within a few days' time. We accomplished our goal by representing all three languages, plus one song to be sung alternating between English and Portuguese. I'm looking forward to regrouping tomorrow so that we can actually do some singing!

Once more I enjoyed dinner this evening in the formal dining room, but honestly... I'm getting kinda tired of eating. How is this possible? I don't know, but it's all I've been doing for the last several days.

I am SO looking forward to arriving in our next port city of Tenerife, Canary Islands in three days. I will walk off this ship and wander the town until I get blisters! My urge to explore has gone unsatisfied for too long, and I'm feeling desperate for some good brisk walking and discovering a new place.

Day 39 - Social Nutrition
Monday, April 18, 2016

When I was twenty years old (many moons ago), I decided to try a little experiment. For an entire week, I ate nothing but Doritos chips, ice cream sandwiches, and peanut butter cups. It was enough to keep me alive and functional, but by the end of the week I didn't feel good at all. I learned that a body can survive on empty calories, but it needs quality nutrition to thrive in good health.

I'm beginning to think that my soul requires similar nutrition in the form of meaningful social interactions. While my fellow passengers on this ship have all been generally friendly and politely sociable... it feels like empty social calories to me. I'm starving for the type of nutritious connections that don't seem to form well in this atmosphere.

Small talk has never been my thing. I thrive on deep, juicy, meaningful conversations that have a lasting impact. In most of my travels, those type of encounters have been suprisingly commonplace.

Even in the candy-coated tourist haven of Blackpool, England, I had an impactful conversation with the owner of the B&B where I stayed, helping him work through some hard feelings around his partner's adopted son. That's the kind of interaction that feeds my soul.

I don't know if it's the language barrier (although I've met plenty of English speakers), the frequent directives from the captain to "enjoy every minute!", or the nature of the individuals who prefer this type of leisure, but I'm just not finding any kindred spirits on this ship.

I think back on the connection I made with the young woman in San Jose, Costa Rica. It took us only minutes to recognize our similarities, which led to hours of deep conversation. That strength of connection isn't quite as common, but I wonder why I struggle so much to form any connections at all around here.

Fortunately, I do get a "vitamin boost" from the relationships forming with my four regular dinner companions. Although they're all longtime friends with each other and there are large differences between our ages, lifestyles, and backgrounds… we've developed genuine caring and interest in each other over our evening meals.

And while we don't dig into juicy topics like philosophy, spirituality, or personal growth; our interactions are genuine. I'm grateful to these four: Frank, Antoinette, Carmen, and Joe.

Day 40 – Bamboozled
Tuesday, April 19, 2016

This morning I had my third and final spa treatment – a bamboo massage. I had never had one of those before, and I imagined something along the lines of a big rolling pin flattening me to the table. Fortunately, the actual treatment was much more gentle and nuanced than my imagination.

The therapist used several different lengths and shapes of bamboo for different areas of my body. The bamboo rods themselves were also heated (like the hot stones in the first massage), helping my muscles melt into the soothing treatment. The shorter rods were perfect for added pressure on shoulders and low back, while the longer rods were great along the muscles of my legs.

But the absolute best part was towards the end of the massage. I was lying face up on the table, when she used one of the longer rods under my neck, and leveraged it up under the base of my skull. Oh, such bliss! I have long term issues with my neck muscles, and have been known to lean up against an empty wine bottle on the back of my sofa to get good pressure in that area.

Somehow I convinced my slackened body to take me back to my room for a shower before lunch. We lost another hour today, as we've done most days on the sea voyage, to assure that we're in alignment with the local time zone when we arrive in the Canary Islands tomorrow. (At long last – we get off the boat!)

I mentioned a few days ago that I've joined a ship's choir, and we had another rehearsal today. The facilitators do an admirable job of leading this multi-national group with a wide range of experience. One gentleman from Austria told me that he's always wanted to sing, but got kicked out of his church choir as a young boy after only one day, and this is the first chance he's had to sing since then. Some have only sung in the shower, while others have had some professional training.

So we all come together with our tri-lingual lyric sheets and do our best to make our way through the four pieces of music we've chosen. We'll have one more one-hour rehearsal before we make our presentation to the rest of the passengers later this week.

After six full days at sea, with really nothing to do but eat and lounge around, I can't even tell you how excited I am to get off the ship and explore Tenerife tomorrow. I've missed walking so much (doing laps around the ship just doesn't cut it), and I'm committed to earning some blisters tomorrow!

Day 41 - Tenerife, Canary Islands, Spain
Thursday, April 21, 2016

After six long (I'm talking LONG) days of nothing but ocean, we finally arrived in the port city of Santa Cruz on the island of Tenerife at 8am yesterday morning. There were several other cruise ships in the large port at the same time and the distance from the gangplank to the city was about one mile. We were offered shuttle busses, but since I was desperate to get out walking anyway, I was more than happy to let my own power carry me the extra distance.

Considering my antsy state from being confined to the ship for a whole week, I knew that I wouldn't respond well to being herded along in another tour group so I set off to explore the city on my own.

Having my feet on solid ground with endless options of which direction to go, what to see, and what to do... I nearly felt like I was flying as I walked briskly up the first interesting avenue I encountered.

The weather was perfect for me – mid 60s, with about 50% cloud cover. The simple joy of walking carried me through the streets for a couple of hours, taking in the locals and tourists alike, as well as taking note of local merchants like the "Banana Store", which was an Apple product reseller. I found my way to the Mercado de Africa (being not so far from the west coast of Morocco) and wandered around perusing vendors of bread, cheese, meat, fish, and trinkets.

I eventually found my way to a museum of natural history. Most of the exhibits were in Spanish only, but with my limited language skills and the multitude of artifacts, I felt both entertained and educated by the experience. As I was getting ready to leave, a large influx of tourists from my boat arrived at the museum and I was glad not to be among the crowd! My wanderings continued into the afternoon, until my body was finally tired enough to return to the ship.

Day 43 - Reflections on the Cruise
Saturday, April 23, 2016

Today is the last day of the cruise and we arrive in Barcelona very early (6am) tomorrow morning. I may have given the impression that I'm not very happy on the boat, which is true in part, but I've also made an effort to remain at least semi-engaged with cruise activities.

I thought back on my very first rustic camp with fellow Druids out in the middle of a cow pasture in rural England in 2004. The conditions were far from luxurious – sleeping on the ground in a large yurt with many other people, sharing one wood-burning shower for the entire camp, the multi-sensory experience of the composting pit toilets – and yet it was one of the happiest times of my life.

I remember truly learning the meaning of "you get out of it what you put into it" at that camp, as I threw myself into many community-building volunteer opportunities and had a great time.

So I wondered how I could put more into my cruise experience, and get more out of it. But the thing is... cruising appears to be purposefully designed as a consumer-only experience.

There was no opportunity to build something together. Nobody asked me to help facilitate or come up with activities for the group. There were no gatherings to honestly share what was going on in our hearts and our minds... just endless "good times." Daily announcements from the captain reminding us to "enjoy every minute, every second!" never failed to irritate me for some reason I couldn't quite pin down.

Finally I saw an item on the daily schedule that caught my interest – passengers were invited to form a ships' choir. At last, something I could contribute! It was a challenge working with people of different languages and varying levels of skill, but I was delighted to take those few hours out of my endless relaxation time and devote my efforts to creating and sharing. We performed four songs for our fellow passengers last night, which gave me great satisfaction.

Later that same night I watched the main show of the cruise – a spectacle of aerial acrobatics along with singing, dancing, and elaborate costuming. And although the show was technically impressive... I didn't feel impressed. I felt that it lacked soul.

Today the crew put on a talent show. The acts were definitely more amateur than last night's spectacle, but I could feel each individual devoting their whole hearts to their performances, and that made all the difference. That amateur talent show was the highlight of the ship's entertainment to me.

There's also value for me in seeing from a new perspective. I mentioned body-image issues in a previous post, and the sites on this ship threw my American sensibilities for a loop. I saw so many soft or rotund bellies exposed around the pool. Bikinis and speed-os showcased impressive rolls, lumps, and bumps like I've never seen before... all of them a shade of deep tan indicating that those bodies are well acquainted with exposure to the light of day.

Part of me wanted to shout, "You go, girl!" to each misshapen bikini body that I saw. Part of me compared my own body to each of them, thinking "if SHE can bare her flabby belly to the world, then so can I!" And part of me was deeply embarrassed that these people didn't have enough shame to hide their imperfections as I've been taught to do in my own culture. (I tried to silence that ugly voice each time it came up, but I can't deny that it exists.)

Its said that still waters run deep, but my experience with the cruise is that deep waters just make me want to dive deeper - to find more substance, and to seek experience beyond the pleasures of simply consuming.

I make no judgements against those who enjoy the many pleasures offered on the ship, but I found that my own satisfaction requires something different than a cruise can provide.

Day 44 - Exploring Barcelona, Spain
Monday, April 25, 2016

The ship docked at 6am in Barcelona. With my belly full from one last breakfast in the ship's dining room, I set off on foot from the pier and found my way to La Rambla, the pedestrian thorough-fare leading from the waterfront into the city, then to the central Plaza Catalunya.

So early on a Sunday morning, all of the other people out and about were dragging luggage with them (just like me), and the city was peaceful and quiet. From the Plaza, I knew that my hostel was northeast and I had a few street names memorized, hop-ing that I'd come upon reassuring checkpoints as I walked.

I definitely had a few moments of fearing that I'd get myself lost (a particular talent of mine), but after 90 minutes of walking I happily found myself at the door to my hostel with no backtrack-ing or going in circles. (Yay me!) I was far too early to check in, but they let me stash my bags so that I could continue my wan-derings unencumbered.

One of the magical things about exploring a new place with no destination in mind is coming upon unexpected wonders. I turned a corner and came face to face with the fantastic façade of Antoni Gaudi's Casa Batlló, pictured here.

It's like coming upon a fairy castle in the middle of the city. Gaudi's style utilizes a lot of tile, stained glass, and organic shaping to the structure that makes it stand out from every other building in the vicinity.

By this time, my body needed

a break from walking and I noticed a hop on/hop off double-decker bus tour getting ready to depart. I bought a two-day pass and boarded the bus for some exploring while resting.

I hopped on and off several times during the day, walking along the waterfront as well. A mall near the marina was the only major commerce open on Sundays, and it was swamped with locals and tourists alike. Toward the evening, I decided it was time to visit a private club that I had researched online in advance.

In my home city of Seattle, recreational marijuana is legal. An increasing number of US states and other locations have been taking steps towards various levels of legalization – Barcelona included.

I was curious to see how Barcelona's emerging "coffee shop" culture compares to Seattle's industry, and so I arranged to join one of the private cannabis clubs in this city. I confirmed that recreational marijuana is indeed legal in Barcelona, just highly regulated and strictly enforced to stay out of public view.

Envisioning myself at a speakeasy in the era of alcohol prohibition, I approached the unmarked door and pressed the buzzer. The door clicked open after a moment and I went into the building lobby looking for the purple door that I was told would be the only indicator of the club entrance. The purple door buzzed open and I entered another lobby where staff assured that I had my membership requirements (photo ID and cash), and then I was warmly welcomed to the club.

After receiving my membership card and purchasing a small portion of sativa-dominant bud (energizing and mildly euphoric) from the half dozen choices on offer, I walked through a series of doors and into the comfortable lounge area. The staff offered me a selection of paraphernalia with which to consume the goods, and assured that my choice was clean and in good working order. All that was left for me to do was take a seat and chill out in the mellow vibe.

There were a dozen other people in the club lounging, chatting, and surfing the free wifi on phones and laptops. For a while I happily stared at the entertaining youtube videos being projected onto the wall, until a couple took seats near me and we struck up a conversation.

In no time at all, we were deep in discussion on topics like the importance of following your dreams and maintaining consciousness in life. I joyfully let my new friends know just how much I had missed exactly that sort of connection while on the ship, and how much I appreciated their camaraderie.

We exchanged contact information and continued enjoying the club until closing time at 9pm, when the three of us left together in search of beer and tapas. We were all still a bit giggly and giddy as we sat down in a nearby restaurant, and had a great time over our food and drink while the remaining effects wore off. We parted for the evening with hugs and hopes to see each other back and the club again.

While the retail marijuana stores of Seattle have much less of a "cloak and dagger" sort of feel, they also lack the social aspect of a place to consume the product and make friends in a safe and cozy atmosphere. I think I really like Barcelona's style!

Day 47 - Works of Gaudí
Wednesday, April 27, 2016

The artistic architectural works of Antoni Gaudí can be found all over Barcelona, and I visited two of his most stunning sites over the last two days. The first was Park Güell, named after Gaudí's partner on their vision of a nature-focused luxury residential area. Only two homes were ever built, and the park now flourishes as a gallery of outdoor architecture.

The site I visited this morning is the famous Sagrada Familia Basilica, which is still under construction decades after Gaudí's death. Both sites were hugely crowded with tourists, which is something I usually try to avoid, but both were also completely worth navigating the hordes of humanity.

There is no single picture that can convey the experience of these artistic masterworks, but the photo below is a partial view of the ceiling on Sagrada Familia. The scalloped columns supporting the structure are modeled after trees, branching out at the top to form a pattern of leaves that allow for sunlight to fall through the skylights above.

Upon entering the basilica, I was overwhelmed with emotion and tears came to my eyes. That was the same reaction I had upon entering the Hypostle (outdoor room with similar tree-like columns) at Park Güell. I can't identify the specific emotions I felt, but I suppose it was simply a visceral response to being in the presence of intense inspiration expressed with such incredible and intricate beauty.

Taking advantage of one of the areas cordoned off for silent reflection and prayer, I took a few minutes to let my tears flow and embrace the overwhelming sensations. I was apparently not the only one deeply affected by the site, because there were others around me also dabbing their eyes and sniffling.

Christian imagery and symbolism are prominently and ornately displayed all over the basilica, inside and out. Scenes of the Nativity, the Passion, and the Glory are featured on the exterior façade on three sides of the structure. Inside there are homages to disciples and saints, as well as crucifixes and vast amounts of stained glass art coloring the incoming daylight.

But despite the presence of so much religious iconography, it felt like a nature temple to me. Gaudi's love of the natural world is just as prominent, expressed as devotion to the creations of God. Outer doors are sculpted with leafy scenes crawling with creatures from snails and spiders to turtles and birds. The attention paid to allowing just the right amount of light and shadow into the sanctuary is apparent, much like walking through a sun-dappled path with a forest canopy above.

Park Güell was a less religious experience and more like walking through the illustrations of Dr. Suess. No straight lines in this park! Every structure has an organic flow and many surfaces are decorated in the broken-tile mosaic style that is emblematic of Gaudí.

A large central square (more of a wavy oval, to be honest) is surrounded on the perimeter by a meandering sculpted mosaic bench overlooking a panoramic view of the city below. The square is supported by the Hypostle columns underneath. Upper walkways around the park are also supported by arching columns below.

No matter where your eye falls in this park, you'll find art and beauty in even the smallest details. The entire site is obviously well-planned to take advantage of the hillside topography, but also has a definite sense of spontaneity. No two of the many, many mosaics are the same, and yet the similarity of style makes it all fit together seamlessly.

Gaudí was obviously a man with a deeply personal spirituality. His expressions of Christianity reflect a devotion to the magic of Creation that makes his art feel accessible to people of many different faiths. As I wandered the sites of his creations, I could only think how much I would have liked to spend some time with the man, basking in the radiance of such an inspired life.

Day 49 - Reflections on Barcelona
Friday, April 29, 2016

As far as cities go, I really like Barcelona. There's a lot to see and do within walking distance from everything else. After days of wandering the city and exploring the works of Gaudí, the rain yesterday gave me a chance to do laundry, upload recent photos, and finish a good book.

I love the art and architecture of this city. I've made friends here and received encouragement to move to the city, but one of the greatest advantages to trying new things is finding the things that *don't* work for you, so that you know to look in other directions.

And as much as I've enjoyed Barcelona, it's just too hard to walk down these streets. It seems that there's always some crowd of people between me and where I want to go - and many of them are openly smoking cigarettes.

I find myself strategically holding my breath as I scan the oncoming foot traffic for smoky puffs, but sometimes I'm trapped behind a burning cigarette until I find another path to dart through the mass of people without being too aggressively pushy. I'm constantly negotiating crowd dynamics, and it's exhausting.

I was grateful to have my membership in the private cannabis club, located right off La Rambla in the center of everything, where I could duck in whenever I needed respite from the crowd, cigarettes, or weather. And it was so convenient for them to hold my luggage after I checked out of my hostel, before I check in for the ferry tonight.

Around 10pm tonight I'll depart on a 20-hour ferry ride from Barcelona to Civitavecchia, a port city about an hour north of Rome. I'll spend tomorrow night in a B&B in Civitavecchia before taking the train into Rome on Sunday to check into a camping village in the city.

Day 51 - Morning in Italia (Civitavecchia, Italy)
Sunday, May 01, 2016

Every once in a while I take a break from the seeing, doing, and experiencing to just BE and sit with the fact that I am in yet another totally new location for me. Its really starting to blow my mind that I just up and decided to go to these places, then did it. This is my life now - an endless wander of endless wonders. (I highly recommend it!)

This morning while I waited a few hours for my train to Rome, I found a shady bench on the seaside to watch the incoming waves, and enjoy the quiet foot traffic of an Italian Sunday morning.

The 21-hour ferry from Barcelona to Civitavecchia was relatively uneventful, although the boat was overrun by noisy teenagers on a school trip. I suspect it was those teens who were running screaming through the corridors from boarding until sunrise, unless Italians in general are even more excitable than I've been led to believe.

Once I managed to separate myself from the disembarking herd, it was a short walk from the pier to the B&B that I had reserved in advance. However, I was dismayed to find the doors closed and locked upon my arrival, with a sign indicating that guests should call the phone numbers provided for check in.

My phone couldn't get through on either number, and I was getting increasingly frustrated when the owner of the restaurant next door came to my rescue. His phone was able to dial the local number that mine couldn't, and he assured me in gestures that someone was coming for me. By that time, both darkness and rain were falling, and so he welcomed me into his space and offered me a chair while I waited.

About 30 minutes later, the property managers showed up and I got settled in my room. Then I went back to the restaurant next door to thank the owner in the best way I knew how – by ordering a meal.

"Chips and Friends" offers the ultimate in comfort food – specializing in french fries, as well as varieties of fried fish and chicken. They also had 20+ different dipping sauces to choose from, which was delightful.

Happily filled with fried food and finally with a place to lay my head for the night, I retired to rest up for my journey into Rome.

Day 52 - Catacombs to Cupola
Monday, May 02, 2016

Today I explored the Vatican from bottom to top (literally!), starting with the Necropolis underneath St. Peter's Basilica, then climbing to the highest point of the dome over the basilica.

I started the morning with a great plan. I could take the earliest 15-minute shuttle from my accommodation to a spot near the Vatican, then walk 30 minutes to get to the Ufficio Scavi (office of excavation) to start the Necropolis tour. Keep in mind that I had to book this limited access tour months in advance, and that there was no late entry allowed.

Knowing that the Vatican is a big place, I scoped it out yesterday so that I wouldn't waste any time getting lost on my way. And then... Monday morning traffic in Rome happened.

I watched the minutes go by as the shuttle inched along, trying to calculate the latest time I could get off the bus and still make it for my 9am tour. Then that time passed, and the shuttle was still in route. (Ack!) Once I recognized the drop-off neighborhood, I asked the driver to let me off and then seriously power-walked the whole way to the Vatican, making my appointment with less than one minute to spare.

With that excitement out of the way, the tour was great. We had a group of fourteen people and got to see the old Roman pagan city under what is now one of the holiest sites in Christendom. We learned about the pagan symbolism still visible in the tile work and the persecution faced by early Christians because of their radical new faith.

The highlight of the tour was learning about the excavation of the bones of St. Peter, who was an apostle of the man now known as Jesus Christ, and actually seeing the bones of the ancient saint through a hole in the "graffiti wall" where they're ensconced. While I'm not Christian myself, the intensity of the historical significance was not lost on me!

During the tour, we were able to look up through decorative grates in the floor above to see the impressive dome of the basilica, so that was my next destination. Not knowing exactly what I was in for, I stood in line for the climb up to the cupola.

Roughly 565 steps later, up an extremely narrow spiral staircase, with the domed walls curving into the head space in places, I arrived at the inside viewing area near the top of the dome.

The view looking down into the basilica with the ant-like people milling around was amazing. Even the immense statues looked miniscule from that height.

But there were more stairs to climb, and so onwards and upwards I went. At long last, I arrived at the upper most viewing point around the outside perimeter of the dome. The views were incredible - when I could fight my way through the crowd clogging the slim viewing deck to the fenced edge for a good look.

Grateful that my knees carried me down all those stairs after going all the way up, I went to explore the ground floor of St. Peter's Basilica.

If I haven't mentioned it before, I really hate crowds. I get so uncomfortable with people in every direction, limiting my movement and vision, and that's exactly the condition that confronted me. I tried wandering for a bit, dodging huge groups of tourists following flag-waving guides. I took in the sculptures and frescoes and marble.

I felt dazed by the opulence. My personal experience of the sacred is usually very subtle – the sound of wind singing through trees, the silent passage of a forest creature across my path, a ray of sunlight at just the right moment. The gold-plated style of sacred displayed in the basilica was foreign to me. There's nothing subtle about the Vatican!

Feeling depleted by the crowds and exhausted by the vast quantity of sacred art all around me, I chose not to fight my way into the Sistine Chapel. Instead, I wandered into the streets of Rome until I found a pizzeria, enjoyed a slice of zucchini pie, and then made my way back to the shuttle pick up point. However, I had failed to note the standard 3-hour Italian lunch period for the shuttle, so I ended up catching a local bus back to my accommodation.

Day 53 - Dem Bones
Wednesday, May 04, 2016

The Capuchin Crypt is a corridor with seven small chambers located beneath the church of Santa Maria della Concezione dei Cappuccini. (Side note: yes, the coffee drink was named after this order, in recognition of the friars' style of a circle of hair around an otherwise bald head, much like the circle of foam on top of a cappuccino.)

When the friars moved into this location, they brought cartloads of bones from about 3,700 deceased monks. The beautiful arrangements of the bones in each room are meant to remind viewers of the inevitability of death, and the importance of living a good (Christian) life.

The installations are gorgeous and fascinating, and not macabre like you might expect. Intricate designs and patterns are created with ribs, metacarpals, skulls, femurs and more. There are chandeliers of vertebrae hanging in some rooms. In one room, a coat of arms is featured on a wall... using actual arms.

Although this is a holy place and photo are forbidden... I saw somebody else take a shot and I couldn't resist the opportunity to capture a few images of my own. I really wanted to share this amazing site with you all, so I hope that the Capuchin friars and the souls of the thousands of deceased people whose bones are on display will forgive my transgression.

Day 54 - When in Rome...
Thursday, May 05, 2016

When in Rome, do as the Romans do, right? But that would mean chain-smoking cigarettes in public, wearing dangerously high heels, and driving like a maniac - not really my style. So maybe do as the tourists do? But that means standing in long lines with huge crowds, clutching my bag to avoid pickpockets. That's no fun either.

My plan was: when in Rome, do as Stef does – book a room outside of the downtown area as close to nature as possible, so that I can have the peace and quiet I need to be able to face the noise and chaos of the city.

But the "camping village" where I stayed is apparently a place where people go to drink and party loudly all night. A toga party paraded past my tent at 2am. No peace and quiet for me. That really put a strain on my ability to deal with the little hassles of life!

After three nights of very little sleep, and three days of serious touristing through intense crowds and trains and subways, I had one final day planned in the city. Even though I probably would have been happier chilling out and reading a book, I chose to go into the city once more for a tour of the Colosseum.

I think I was experiencing what's known as FOMO (fear of missing out) – thinking of how people would react knowing that I had been in Rome and hadn't visited every famous and important site – so I went.

That poor choice led to my first stress-fueled mini-meltdown of the journey so far. This is a reminder to me that my first priority must be to meet my own needs, not to worry about how other people will judge my choices. (Isn't that a lesson for all of us?)

I had also made plans to meet a new friend for lunch in the city before the afternoon tour. I walked to the train station to get myself into the city, confident that I knew what I was doing since I had taken the exact same route the day before. I got there with plenty of time to spare, because I get very anxious about being late.

After standing around for quite some time, I wondered why the train would be so late. Then it dawned on me that the train I needed to take had already departed from a different platform. (D'oh!)

I messaged my friend to let him know I wouldn't be able to make our lunch, and sat down miserably to wait for the next train an hour later. I was kicking myself for not thinking to check the details, and feeling on the verge of tears for making such a stupid mistake. I also realized that I would be cutting it very close to get to my pre-paid tour on time, and was feeling more and more stressed.

My friend still wanted to meet to at least say goodbye before I left the city, but the train station is huge and crowded and I could feel those minutes I needed slipping away as we tried to find each other.

When we finally did connect, I was in no mood to be with people – stormy with stress and unable to even crack a smile. The poor man wanted to help me, but all I really needed was time and space on my own to cool down.

In the end, I did get to my tour on time, and even had time for a very quick bite to eat (hunger wasn't helping my mood.) But my attitude still needed adjusting in order to avoid glaring at my fellow tour participants, so I found a friendly nearby tree to help.

Trying not to be conspicuous on a busy street corner, I stood connected to the Italian Pine tree with my eyes closed and slowed my breathing until I felt capable of dealing with people again.

The tour was informative and the sites impressive, but I was still tired and cranky on the inside, and was ready to be done about halfway through the four-hour walk. Again, I was reminded that in the future I need to make choices to support my own well-being, not push myself to do what "everybody does". If I do something for the wrong reasons, I'm not likely to feel very good about it anyway!

So the moral of this story is: when in Rome... honor yourself and your own needs, no matter what the Romans are doing.

Day 57 - Kissos, Greece
Saturday, May 07, 2016

My journey away from the chaos of Rome involved a forty-minute shuttle, a two-hour plane ride, a one-hour bus ride, an overnight hotel stay, another two and a half hours by coach through winding mountain roads overlooking incredible views, and finally a five-minute walk from the tiny village of Kissos. Now I'm in an enchanted area of amazing greenery, with stunning views of the ocean from the heights of Mt. Pelion. Ah, bliss!

I'm at one of three properties of the Kalikalos community and retreat center. They'll open for guests and workshops in a month, but until then... there's a lot of work to be done to clean up and prepare. Although there was technically a caretaker at the Kissos property over the last seven months, they didn't take good care of the place and it shows.

The single room that I had booked was not yet cleaned, so I spent the afternoon sweeping cobwebs from the walls and ceiling, dusting the furniture, vacuuming the mattress, sweeping the stone floor, finding fresh sheets and reasonably clean blankets, then finally making my bed. The en suite bathroom was a more daunting task, so I just wiped down the sink and toilet, trying to avoid looking at the shower.

By 8:30pm, the other guests/volunteers had arrived, along with several people from the other two properties of Kalikalos, and our welcome dinner was ready to be served. About two dozen of us sat down to a meal of spaghetti with tomato/veggie sauce, salad, fresh bread, and locally made red wine. The evenings get cold this high in the mountains, and we were all bundled up as we enjoyed our dinner in the outdoor courtyard between the kitchen and the guest house.

It was time for bed once dinner and clean up was completed, so I returned to my room to burrow under a pile of blankets for a cold, but cozy night's sleep. I was thinking back on the movie "Under the Tuscan Sun", where a woman buys a dilapidated old estate in Italy and sets out to restore it. This old stone manor in Greece feels much like that situation, but at least we have fresh clean running water and passable internet access!

This morning we got a slow start, since there's still so much cleaning and unpacking to do, but eventually got around to preparing and eating a simple breakfast of oatmeal, fruit, seeds and nuts. Following breakfast, we had our first community meeting of the season, with several rounds of passing the "talking stick" around the circle so that each person had the opportunity to share their thoughts and feelings. Eventually we got around to discussing the rules and guidelines of the center, with the caveat that anything can be changed with good reason.

There was a definite intention to get some work done today, and a few things were indeed accomplished, but for the most part we newly arrived volunteers just got a tour of the property.

During the tour, we found the checklist to be followed for meal procedures, just in time to prepare lunch. More cleaning, unpacking, finding things, and generally trying to figure out what

should be done followed, before enjoying a simple lunch of tomatoes, cucumbers, lettuce, olives (oh, how I love the olives!), more
fresh bread, and feta cheese.

After lunch, people went to the beach or to hike to a nearby waterfall, and I went with the latter group. The greenery of this mountain paradise is stunning – and apparently a rarity in Greece. As
we hiked along the dirt road (with not even one car in the 90+
minutes I was out there), we were treated to stunning views of the
ocean with miles of trees stretching out to the water.

The majority of people at Kalikalos have some connection to the
community that I visited in Scotland in 2005, Findhorn. We all
share a lot of common interests along the lines of community and
spirituality, and its great fun to discover our similar experiences.
I spoke to one man who even felt much like I had when he took a
cruise – being bored with all the 'fun' and unable to connect with
fellow passengers.

I think there are some definite challenges ahead of me here (on a
number of levels), but also a lot of great opportunities. More on
that later!

Day 61 - Meeting Needs
Wednesday, May 11, 2016

Communities can be incredible sources of support and sustenance for their members, but like any relationship, communities
have an abundance of needs that must be met in order to remain
healthy and functional. Additionally, each and every individual
who is part of a community has his/her own unique needs that
also must be fulfilled. The tricky part, of course, is finding that
careful balance wherein everyone's individual needs are met,
along with the needs of the community as a whole.

Five days into my temporary membership in this community and
I'm already struggling with that balance. The needs of the property where this month-long work camp is being held are intense
after seven months of winter dormancy. Lots of physical labor is
required, and huge amounts of cleaning are necessary - and all

the scrubbing in the world still won't return many items to the pristine condition that my perfectionist tendencies long to see.

Although this is most definitely an international community – representing individuals from at least eight different countries – the daily schedule mostly reflects the local Greek lifestyle. The day starts with a light casual breakfast followed by a 60-90 minute community meeting. We work for a few hours, then break for lunch at 1:30pm. When lunch is cleaned up, then we take the next few hours to enjoy the beach or pursue other personal activities (like blog writing). We come back together in the evening for another work shift, breaking for the main meal of the day at 8pm.

That schedule is radically different than my preferred style of expending most of my productive energy in the beginning of the day, relaxing when the work is done, and then enjoying an earlier dinner with social activities in the evening.

I find myself struggling to maintain my emotional balance with the physical demands of the work, the unnatural (to me) schedule, and my strong desire to be a positive contributing member of the community. I love the amazing people I'm living and working with, and I want to be a warm and supportive presence for each of them, but that's also difficult when I'm having such challenges managing my own moods.

My struggles are compounded by the very basic accommodations, when my preference is always for a higher degree of comfort. My bed is warm and clean enough to allow me to sleep, but small and nowhere near the lush comfort of my bed at home.

And while I'm grateful for my own private bathroom, used toilet paper must be collected in a bin rather than flushed (a bin that I'm responsible for emptying), and there's no way to use the handheld shower without making a wet mess of the room (which I then have to mop up). Hot water is also very limited in quantity, and only available for a couple of hours in the morning and again in the evening.

So my needs for physical and environmental comfort are being seriously challenged, while I'm trying hard to relax my need for control over my own daily rhythm. And I find myself wondering how I can manage the whole two weeks to which I've committed, also recognizing that I am unwilling to abandon this community of people and their mission.

One of the hardest things for me to do is ask for help. However, that seems to be the clear answer to my dilemma – to reach out for the support of the community that I am devoting so much of my energy to supporting.

Part of me believes that I should "suck it up" and rally forth with stoicism to simply get the job done, putting my own needs on the back burner until I can take care of myself later. But the wiser part of me recognizes that relegating my personal needs doesn't truly serve the greater good, since that choice only leaves me depleted and unable to lend my unique talents to the cause.

Open honest communication is the foundation of any healthy relationship – including the complex dynamic of community. So I reach out to express my needs – slowly and carefully because such communication makes me feel vulnerable and exposed.

These people care about me as an individual as much as they care about the community and the work we do here. I have to put my trust in others as much as they put their trust in me, and perhaps in that way, all of our needs can be met.

Day 64 - Change of Venue
Saturday, May 14, 2016

When last I wrote, I was struggling with the intensity of work to be done and a lower level of comfort than I need to maintain my positive mood. Even though I expressed my feelings quietly, my plea was heard and the community shifted to accommodate me – moving my efforts to another area of need.

Last night I moved from the more rustic location in the village of Kissos, down the mountain a ways to the more luxurious accommodation of the Alexandros Hotel. My work assignment is now "home care" (sweeping, laundry, general tidiness) of this property that is currently hosting 8-10 staff and retreat guests. I also continue helping to prepare and clean up meals, as everyone in the community does.

My previous room was in a cold dark basment where I huddled under several blankets every night. My new room is warm and bright on the top floor, with a balcony overlooking the sea. The sound of ocean waves below are carried on the breeze. The Agean Sea, which is a shade of aquamarine I had never experienced before, is just a twenty-minute walk away.

Being surrounded by comfort and beauty makes waking up to face the work day a pleasure rather than a chore. Added to the more gentle work requested of me here, my mood is rising higher by the hour.

I'm still part of the same community and still practicing the concept of work as love in action. The major difference for me is that I feel good – so I smile and connect with others more, and am better able to offer my unique gifts of presence and listening in addition to my assigned tasks. When I didn't feel good, I avoided eye contact, wasn't able to call up a genuine smile, and didn't have the energy to offer my gifts where I felt they were needed.

Much like the lesson I learned in Rome (to do things my own way, no matter what I perceive may be expected of me), I've learned here that I must honor my own needs in order to be truly present.

I'm letting go of the idea that one must suffer to be of service. When I try to fill needs that I'm not truly suited to filling, I only damage myself. (If you use a hammer to chop down a tree, you're only going to break the hammer.) The greatest value that I can contribute is through using my strengths joyfully, not through punishing myself for my weaknesses.

One of the joys of community is that there's opportunity for everyone to contribute in their own way. I'm grateful that this community of Kalikalos values what I have to offer, and cares enough to help me maintain my own happiness.

Day 68 – Community
Wednesday, May 18, 2016

My time in the community of Kalikalos is coming to an end in two days. It feels a little strange to be leaving when I feel so invested in the people and the place, but I knew all along that my journey would continue onward after only two weeks.

I've been made very welcome here and assured that my contributions are valued. Encouragement to return has been abundant. The heart connections I've made with so many individuals here make it hard to leave and those same connections may draw me back to this place in the future.

As a fiercely independent individual with strong tendencies toward being a loner, it's been challenging for me to spend so much time with others. I share every meal (including cooking and cleaning) with the community, in addition to working together several hours every day.

In our free time, we tend to play together as well. The only time I spend alone is sleeping in my room at night – and even that is a rarity here where many people share accommodations. Its a huge shift from my usual lifestyle of spending most of the time with only my own company.

When on my own, I'm incredibly efficient. I finish my tasks quickly and am always on time for the next item on my schedule. When in a community, that just isn't possible. I must bend and flow with the ever-changing and often-conflicting needs of the people around me.

This isn't bad or good, simply the inevitable result of different streams of energy and intention converging. Even when we're working towards the same stated goals, we all have our own ways of attempting to achieve our ideas, and we can easily get in each other's way.

But with all of these challenges come great rewards as well. There is no individual among us (certainly not me!) who could build or maintain this center on their own. To achieve great things, we absolutely MUST work together, and find our way through the many intricate issues to forge a path forward towards our shared vision of creation. The greatest accomplishments of humanity (some of which I've had the privilege to witness on my journey so far) have required the combined efforts of countless individuals.

At the same time that I'm diving into this community in Greece, I hear that the communities I've left behind back home are struggling. My beloved monthly community drum circle has come to an end with the leadership needing to shift energy to other projects. My beloved community of local Druids seems to be struggling as there aren't enough interested attendees to hold our previously popular annual retreat. I'm left wondering if continuing to contribute my energy to those communities could have made a difference, and if withdrawing my energy to focus on my own project has had a detrimental impact.

I continue pondering that careful balance between the needs of individuals and the needs of community. I suppose that's a very large question that societies have been debating since the first humans came together. The question is evident from the microcosm of nuclear family dynamics to the grand scale of international politics. How much value do we place on the needs of the individual, and how much do we place on the needs of the community as a whole – the "greater good?"

Is there some way that serving the needs of oneself as an individual can also support the needs of the whole? I don't know. That does seem to be an idealistic answer to a deeply complex question, and perhaps more of a dream than a real solution... but hey, I'm a dreamer!

What I do know is that my presence makes an impact wherever I choose to devote my energy. My contributions add value, and my support makes a difference. (I suspect that much is true for every individual, whether they can see that truth or not.)

And so I'll continue forward with my journey, taking the lessons I'm learning and trying to forge that knowledge into the wisdom to make beneficial choices as I move through life. I'll continue to make heart connections with other individuals, and continue to meet my own needs, and hope somehow to serve the greater good along the way.

Day 71 - In Transit
Saturday, May 21, 2016

Today I write my blog on a bus bound for Athens. I arrived in Volos last night after a rainy two-hour bus ride down Mount Pelion from the Kalikalos community. As soon as the bus entered the city to encounter traffic, people, and noise... I missed the tranquility of the mountain.

Although I only spent one night in Volos two weeks ago, it felt really good to arrive somewhere relatively familiar. I knew the way to my hotel from the bus station, knew where to get cash, and I even knew where to find a good souvlaki stand for some quick take-away dinner. There was no anxiety, no uncertainty - just total efficiency in taking care of business so that I could settle in for some much needed rest.

It also feels familiar to be back on my own again, but I do miss the warm embrace (literally!) of the community around me. I miss the quiet camaraderie of nodding hello to friends during the morning period of silence. I miss the incredible, tasty, healthy food prepared by our talented cooks. I miss the open sharing of feelings during our daily meetings. I miss the soul satisfaction of practicing "work as love in action" in community.

But even though I share portions of this trip with friends and family, the journey is mine alone. It's only my own motivation that propels me from destination to destination, forging ahead into the unknown after a brief respite of comfort and familiarity.

I'm looking forward to these next four days in Athens, taking in the amazing history and vibrancy of a city both ancient and modern. I'll balance my adventuring with taking care of my needs for quiet and solitude. As much as I'd love to do and see "everything" that Athens has to offer, I'll choose carefully so that I leave feeling both fulfilled and energized.

And then I go ever further outside of my comfort zone, finally departing from "the western world." On Wednesday I fly from Athens, through Qatar, and into the rural southwest of India.

I'm nervous about spending my 8-hour layover in Qatar airport, not knowing what expectations there may be of a solo female traveler in the Middle East. I don't know if I should cover my head, or avoid eye contact with men, or just hide in a corner until my connecting flight is ready to board.

So I take these last four days in relatively familiar comfort, preparing myself for the unknown to come. The people of the world are almost always friendly, welcoming, and eager to help a traveler in need. All I have to do is smile and do my best to communicate my needs and someone will try to help.

And on a sad note, a member of my extended family lost his battle with cancer a couple days ago. His passing leaves a hole in our family.

My heart aches for his wife of 50 years, their children and grandchildren as they mourn his loss. Its difficult to be so far away when my family is suffering such grief.

Rest in peace, Joe. You are greatly loved and greatly missed.

Day 72 - Fish Food (Athens, Greece)
Sunday, May 22, 2016

Sometimes you eat the fish… sometimes the fish eat you.

After a walking tour of Athens this morning, I decided to indulge in a foot massage followed by a "fish spa." The top-rated Athens Fish Spa offers a variety of spa services, including four individual tanks of *garra rufa* fish, which consume the dead skin from the feet of spa-goers.

The spa itself was serene and comfortable, asking clients to show up significantly early to relax and enjoy tea before services begin. When it was time, my technician scrubbed my feet before taking me back to a warm dark room with a lounge chair and propping my legs up on a padded ottoman. I laid back and relaxed while he worked magic on my overused tootsies and lower legs for 50 minutes.

When the massage was over, he led me back out to the main room (where the fish spa tanks are prominently displayed), and I washed my feet once more before submerging them to the mercy of the fishies.

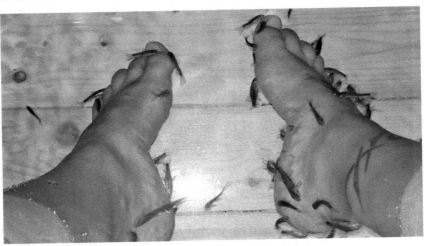

I'll admit that I did squeal at the first enthusiastic touch of the dozens of tiny creatures rushing to feast on my bounty of dead skin, but the sensation soon mellowed out to nothing more than a slight tingle. I watched the whole time, fascinated by the fish wriggling around my toes and nibbling on my ankles. And after 20 minutes, my feet were baby-bottom soft, just as advertised.

The walking tour this morning was great as well, arranged as a free service by the hostel where I'm staying. We had a group of 20+ people, and our guide did an admirable job of herding us along, and across several treacherous intersections. (Don't even get me started on the chaos that is Greek traffic. It's too scary to talk about!)

We learned some history and mythology along the way. I now know that a marathon is exactly 42.195km because that is the exact distance that a single injured soldier ran after the battle of Marathon, to warn and therefore save the people of Athens before the Persians attacked.

The unnamed soldier collapsed and died as soon as his warning was uttered, and the marathon then became an event in the Olympics to commemorate that soldier's incredible feat of strength and endurance.

The tour also took us to the Panathenaic Stadium (where the first modern Olympic Games were held in 1896), and to the unfinished temple of Zeus and other sites.

More to see, more to do, and more to eat tomorrow! (Have I mentioned how much I love Greek food...?)

Day 74 - Reflections on Greece
Tuesday, May 24, 2016

I love Greece. The people are warm and welcoming, the land and sea produce infinite shades of blue and green, and the food is so fresh and tasty! The rural areas of Mount Pelion are amazingly beautiful and reflect the laid back character of its inhabitants.

Athens is steeped in history, but I'm a little embarassed to admit that I've started feeling a bit blasé about ancient ruins. ("Hey cool, that's really old and crumbly... what else ya got?")

111

The Acropolis was my first stop for exploration yesterday, since it had been beckoning to me from the hilltop visible from my roof-top terrace. It was big and impressive with lots of columns, and a great view of the amphitheater that's still used today for live performances. It was also very crowded with tourists and baking under relentless sunshine with no shade to be had.

After dutifully taking my photos and stumbling across the many uneven mounds of smooth marble poking up from the ground – thwarting even my rugged Teva sandals from gaining traction – I exited the site in search of water and shade.

Athens is a living city and there is so much more going on than just relics of the past. I found the nearest vendor along the tourist thoroughfare named after the god of wine, theater, and general good times (Dionysus) and got myself a cold bottle of water.

Then I found a shady spot to sit and listen to one of the many street musicians. That set the pattern for the rest of my day as I continued wandering down the long pedestrian way, stopping to listen and leave tips to help support the many street musicians.

I'm always happy to support street performers, but I never support the scam artists who use deceit or manipulation to take advantage of good-hearted people. I've encountered plenty of the latter in my travels so far, many of whom can be very aggressive.

From the children with sad expressions sitting with their grubby hands out, to the flower ladies shoving "free" blossoms at passersby and then demanding money, to the African woman who insisted on gifting me with "free" trinkets of her homeland – only to come back a few minutes later asking for money to support her children, and then take back the trinkets when I wouldn't give her money.

Greece is still suffering from economic woes and many individuals are struggling as well. Neighborhoods look shabby – covered in graffiti to the point that it looks abandoned when the storefronts are closed. But when the stores are open, the streets come alive. Shopkeepers move their wares to the entrances and people passing by stop to chat as they go about their business.

I never saw police when I was on the mountain, but I've seen a handful around the tourist area in Athens where I'm now staying. In any highly trafficked area, I always take security precautions – assuring that my hand is on my "travel-safe" bag at all times, and practicing conscious awareness of my surroundings. I haven't had even one moment of feeling unsafe in this city... unless you count trying to cross the street.

I'm told that a recent strike by bus drivers in Athens made the traffic worse than usual, but the haphazard style of Greek driving can't be accounted for just from that factor alone. Cars can be parked 2-3 deep at the curb, and some of them park at odd angles sticking into the street.

Drivers dart around the parked cars, whip around blind corners at impossible angles (the streets don't resemble a grid by any stretch of the imagination), but generally try to avoid colliding with pedestrians or anything else. Cross walks and lights appear to be few and far between. My best strategy was to wait at a corner until a group of people made a move into the street. (They can't hit all of us at once, right?)

And the food... oh, the food... I have eaten very well in this country. Grilled skewers of chicken and pork served with pita, tzatziki and veggies (souvlaki); fresh fish, local beef meatballs, salads of eggplant and beetroot, copious amounts of fresh baked bread with olive oil and vinegar... and baklava. (Yum!) Yesterday I even had ice cream made with baklava in it. These people are genius!

Tomorrow I move on to India, with a new set of challenges and all new people, places and food to explore. The journey continues!

Day 76 - Arrival in India
Friday, May 27, 2016

In the Qatar airport there was such a variety of international travelers that I felt completely comfortable as a solo American woman in western attire. I couldn't resist trying the Middle Eastern version of an American classic, the Burger King Whopper, at the airport food court.

I was feeling so at home that it was then a bit surprising to find that I was the only female on the plane not dressed in a full burka. (There is a significant population of Muslims in India, as well as Christians and Hindus.)

They appeared to be some sort of emergency aid group traveling together, most of them carrying matching red bags, and the women all wearing matching (hot pink) head scarves branded with what I assumed was the name of their organization. I managed to make eye contact and smile with a few of the women, but for the most part we basically ignored each other, unsure of how to interact given our obvious differences.

Upon landing in India, the weather hit me like a ton of hot wet bricks. India is currently experiencing an unusual heat wave with temperatures in the mid-90s accompanied by thick humidity.

Although I flew into a relatively small airport, the crowd gathered outside waiting for loved ones was still a bit overwhelming to me. However, I managed to connect with my pre-arranged taxi and we set off into the adventure that is driving in India.

There's a line down the center of the road that appears to divide it into two reasonably sized lanes, one for traffic in each direction. But in reality... those two lanes become more like six – as cars, trucks, auto-rickshaws, scooters, and pedestrians all dart in and out of line, honking and trying to find the quickest path through thick congestion.

Women in their long colorful dresses were riding side-saddle behind men driving scooters, but that wasn't as surprising as seeing an entire family of four crammed onto a single scooter - with mom perched precariously side-saddle on the rear.

Three hours of heart-stopping traffic, nine hair-pin mountain switchbacks, one roadside monkey, and a rugged country road later, I arrived at my destination of Greenex Farms.

I was greeted with a glass of fresh made lemonade before being welcomed to sit down for a lunch of tasty chicken biriyani. After enjoying my lunch, I was shown to my tree house and left to relax until tea time. Although the treehouse doesn't have air conditioning, I was comfortable enough with a fan to take a short nap in the heat of midday.

I wandered back through the meandering trails of the property to the restaurant for tea, where I met the owner of Greenex Farms. Teddy and I chatted over our chai and banana fritters, and then he offered to give me a tour of the property. In the outside world he's an entrepreneur with projects in many large Indian cities, but here in this mountain paradise of lush green jungle, Teddy is a visionary.

In only eight short years, he has transformed this rustic remote property into a model of eco-sustainability and managed to enhance the already astounding natural beauty. All power to the site is solar, and much of the food served in the restaurant is grown in the gardens here. What food can't be grown on the property is collected daily from local organic sources. Many of the staff live on-site in family dwellings or bachelor quarters.

Each of the eleven unique guest accommodations was designed and built by Teddy, with the exception of the original 2-bedroon mud-walled farmer's cabin that came with the property. The elementally themed dining, swimming, and play areas were all constructed from his imagination and the suggestions of guests over the years – including a shallow river with handmade bamboo rafts that guests can row.

A couple of hours after the glorious sunset, it was time for dinner on the fire-themed terrace. The perimeter is lined with candles in beautiful sconces, and a bonfire is prepared near the dining tables.

I had ordered my choices for dinner in advance (gobi manchurian and matar paneer), which were both excellent. In addition, they gave me a lentil dish, and some yogurt to help cut the spiciness and soothe my unaccustomed taste buds. A special beverage is served to guests - water boiled with an herb to aid digestion - and

I consumed huge amounts of the warm pink-tinted liquid.

Teddy and his wife Anita were present for dinner, and we all enjoyed great conversation along with one other guest from France. We were also served a light dessert of gulab jammun (small pastry ball in sugar syrup) to remove any lingering discomfort from the spices of dinner.

I then retired to my tree house for the night, and enjoyed the music of the jungle all around me. The birds, insects, frogs, and who knows what else all joined together in a chorus to serenade the stars overhead as I drifted into peaceful slumber.

Day 78 - Settling In
Saturday, May 28, 2016

My first morning in the tree house, I awoke to the sound of birds chirping and a tiny lizard on my doorstep. I wandered to the restaurant for a cup of chai followed by a breakfast of scrambled eggs masala and toast with butter and jam. After breakfast I took a walk through some of the property's trails, and made my way to the Aqua area, where I relaxed reading my book sitting on a lounge chair overlooking the swimming pond.

I floated through my first full day at Greenex Farms, alternating between lounging and showing up for super tasty meals. The property owner, Teddy, has been great about making recommendations for food selections and assuring that the meals aren't too spicy for my western taste buds to enjoy.

Every meal has been incredibly fresh, well prepared and presented. The kitchen staff has also kept me supplied with to-go bottles of the boiled herbal water, assuring that my digestive system stays happy!

When I returned to the tree house after lunch, I found a pack of monkeys waiting for me. There must have been at least 20 of the small primates hanging out under the house and in the surrounding trees... but every single one of them was camera shy. They would stand still as long as I was just staring at them, but the moment I reached for my camera, they bolted every time. I spent the afternoon lounging on my deck and being entertained by the monkeys playing in the trees.

At tea time I said goodbye to the monkeys and headed back to the Aqua area, where I enjoyed conversation with the owner and fellow guests, as well as some chai served with onion pakoras and banana fritters. Next I tried lounging in one of the hammocks for a while before heading back to the tree house to rest after a long day of relaxing.

Several more guests arrived in the afternoon, so dinner on the Flames terrace was even more festive than the first night. My ginger chicken and veggie cutlets were both very tasty (of course), and the atmosphere was friendly and fun. As I was calling it a night, some of other the other guests were putting on some music and showing off their best Bollywood dance moves.

For my second day, we made arrangements for a jeep driver to take me off the property and show me around the Wayanad district. First stop was the Banassura Dam – one of the largest mud-built (power generating) dams in all of Asia. It was obviously a popular destination for local tourists, with many families and large groups wandering around.

However, it seems that Western foreigners are a rarity in this area and I felt like an exotic creature spotted in the wild with all of the attention in my direction. A little boy came close to me with obvious interest, but ran away before making contact.

Later, a little girl boldly came up to say hello with a big smile and shake my hand before giggling and running back to her father. I made sure to make a lot of eye contact, smile, and say hello to people often in passing. I've found the locals to be very friendly and welcoming, once they know that the same is true of me.

Our next stop was the Sooji Para Waterfalls. This was also a popular destination with the locals, many of whom were bathing (fully clothed) and washing clothes in the clear mountain water. My driver, Thomas, and I waded into a small pool ourselves to enjoy the refreshingly cool water after the sweaty walk around the Dam.

We continued climbing up the mostly dry stones of the nearly empty riverbed leading to the slow trickle of the falls. This region has been experiencing a drought and water levels are nowhere near where they should be at this time of year, but the area was still beautiful and well worth the effort to climb to the top.

The weather forecast led me to expect rain and stormy weather throughout my entire weeklong visit here, given that this is the beginning of monsoon season, but its been mostly sunny with just a few rolling booms of thunder and only a couple of brief sprinkles. There was some promising wind and lightning when I returned after my touring this afternoon, but still no downpour of rain.

I'm planning another day of relaxation on the property for tomorrow. Its so peaceful and pleasant here. I'm totally content to simply sit quietly and let my senses take in all the activity of the jungle around me.

In times of stress I remind myself to breathe, and now I can call up the memory of breathing this clean fresh mountain air to calm my stresses in the future. Ah, bliss!

Day 79 - Free to Grow
Sunday, May 29, 2016

The robust tree next to me in this photo is a ficus. You know those spindly little potted trees so common in offices and shopping malls, which are usually barely bigger than a houseplant? Yea, that kind of ficus. And the one in this photo was planted only eight years ago.

I've never seen another ficus in the wild, so maybe this one isn't so big, but in comparison to so many indoor ficus that I've encountered... this one is more than giant, especially considering its young age.

I suspect that the tremendous growth of this tree was supported by the spring directly beneath its roots, and the abundance of daily sunshine in the Indian climate. But even more, this tree is free to grow with wild abandon, unlike its more domesticated counterparts that are forever trapped in pots.

I started to feel a kinship with this tree, having only recently freed myself from my own potted existence. Before leaving my previous domestication, I did grow as a person, just not at the accelerated pace that I'm enjoying with my newfound freedom.

Much like the potted indoor ficus, I was able to remain relatively healthy and stable in the protected environment of my day to day life. I didn't suffer for lack of food or shelter. I had easy access to everything I needed to sustain my basic needs... but was also limited by the container (job, home, etc.) that provided for those same needs.

When I gave up my comfortable domesticated life to embark on this journey, I removed myself from the pot, so to speak. Instead of regimented daily waterings and artificial light, I am now fed by the limitless wellspring of my own imagination, and nurtured by the bright illumination of experiences and friendships that I collect along the way.

I can feel my own roots growing deeper into the earth – becoming stronger and more stable as I gain confidence in myself - even as I thrive in the freedom to move around the planet.

But I also recognize that living in the wild comes with risks as well as rewards. An office ficus is far less likely to suffer the effects of pests, blight, and natural disasters. Living in the wild means being exposed to certain dangers, but facing those dangers also means reaping the rewards of greater resilience in the long term.

And so I continue letting my branches reach ever higher into the sky, unfolding new leaves to capture ever more sunlight to sustain my growth, and reveling in the strength of my deepening roots. It's good to be in the wild, a part of nature, and a part of this world.

Day 80 - Going Native
Monday, May 30, 2016

One of the things I love best about India is the incredibly colorful, beautiful clothing worn by the women. I couldn't leave the country without a shopping trip, so after some site-seeing in the morning, I asked my driver to take me to Kalpetta where he delivered me to the finest textile shop in town.

The store called Sindur contains four stories of Indian fashions, along with plenty of shoppers and staff sifting through it all. Even though some English is spoken, it still took a phone call to my accommodation to help communicate what I was looking for to the shop staff. Once we all understood that I was looking for the long tunic top and trousers that are common attire in this region, we were all set.

Although the clothing is ready-made, it isn't displayed on racks like in American shops. Instead, the garments are folded and kept on shelves behind a counter that wraps around the entire perimeter of the store, with dozens of staff behind it to pull items down and show them to customers. A girl came by to offer me some chai, and a chair was pulled up so that I could look at my options in comfort.

They started pulling down tunics for me and trying to gauge sizes. There was an amazing assortment of colors and patterns to choose from, some of which went beyond even my intense love for the bright and the bold. I eventually took a stack of tunics into the dressing room to see what fit best.

Sadly, I found that the American fascination with adding a bit of spandex to every item of clothing hasn't hit India yet. Every single garment was too tight around my chest with no give whatsoever in the fabric. (Alas!)

I tried several more items, but not one of them fit me right. I gave up on the idea of that style of outfit and went down the stairs to the floor devoted to sarees.

A saree is the more traditional Indian clothing, which is simply a few yards of decorated fabric that is artfully wrapped and draped around the body to resemble a long dress. A very short blouse and underskirt are traditionally worn underneath.

As I've come to expect, I was quite a spectacle in the shop as an obvious foreigner. By the time that one woman had helped wrap me up in my chosen saree, we had attracted the attention of about a dozen other shop girls who gathered around to stare smiling at the unusual site of a white woman in Indian garb.

In the end, my purchase of the saree and a shiny gold half-blouse came to about 1700 rupees, or around $25. I won't have much occasion to wear it back home, but that's a very reasonable price for such an authentic souvenir and I feel good about supporting a local merchant.

Day 81 – One Last Day at Greenex
Tuesday, May 31, 2016

I spent my final day at Greenex Farms relaxing and enjoying the hammocks, birds, monkeys, and abundant variety of plant life. And when darkness fell… Nature put on a farewell finale for me.

The view from my balcony stretched over the rolling tea bush-covered hills, with mountains punctuating the horizon in the distance. Every evening I had seen a few flashes behind the mountains after dark, but on my last night there was a major light show.

There was no rain overhead, but I could hear occasional claps of thunder, and the wind was whipping through the tall thin trees all around me. When I started noticing the bright flashes, I turned out the lights in my room, pulled a chair onto my deck, and sat back to take it all in.

There were thick clouds hovering over the distant mountains, and each strobe flash of lightning lit up the sky and highlighted the multi-layered outline of the clouds. In between flashes, I was entertained by the comparatively soft blinking lights of fireflies flitting through the jungle around me. It was a great send-off!

Day 82 – A Very Long Drive
Wednesday, June 01, 2016

After a lovely farewell breakfast at Greenex Farms, the taxi arrived to transport me the 275km to the city of Kochi for my departing flight the following day. We departed around 10am and encountered the typical traffic of India for most of the ride.

We stopped a few times seeking out an ATM that would accept my debit card, first finding machines for locals only, which require a

6-digit PIN and have a limit of 1000 rupees ($15) per transaction when I needed 8000 to pay for my ride. We eventually found a machine that took my card and gave me enough cash, and we were back on the road.

About seven hours later, after stopping to ask probably a dozen locals for directions along the way, we found the airport hotel that I booked to make my early morning flight easier. By that time the monsoon had descended and the rain was impressive, so I ordered room service and cozied up with my high speed internet for the night.

Day 83 - Currency Exchange
Thursday, June 02, 2016

By this time, I've visited nine different countries, represented by seven different currencies. I've kept a coin or two from each location along the way, since it's rare that I purchase actual souvenirs and the coins are light enough to avoid weighing down my bags.

This morning I departed from India, where local currency isn't allowed out of the country – meaning that I needed to exchange whatever cash I had left before departure, since no currency exchange outside of India can accept rupees. But of course, there was no option available to exchange rupees for the Malaysian ringgits of my next destination, so I opted for euros instead.

Once my Air Asia flight was off the ground, the cabin stewards came by with food for purchase. They said they could accept rupees or ringgits, but not my Visa card. I had less than a dollar's worth of rupees left, and zero ringgits, and I was already hungry at the beginning of my four-hour flight. Uh oh.

So we started negotiating: "Do you have US dollars?" Only in my checked luggage, in the belly of the plane. "Will you accept my euros?"

After a consult with the head flight attendant and some quick work on a calculator, they took my ten euro note and loaded me up with extra snacks, handing back a few ringgits in change. Sometimes you gotta be flexible if you want to eat!

Day 84 – Exploring Kuala Lumpur, Malaysia
Saturday, June 04, 2016

On my first full day in Kuala Lumpur (or KL, as those in the know call it), I visited the Batu Caves, just outside of the city. The caves are a naturally spectacular formation and the local people recognized the site as sacred, building temples inside and around them.

I've found KL an easy city to navigate, and getting there involved only a short walk and a 20-minute train ride directly to the Caves. After leaving the train and making my way through a gauntlet of sidewalk vendors, I climbed the 272 stairs to the entrance of the main cave. (Ironically, there was a "no exercising" sign posted where we all huffed and puffed our way up the stairs.)

There were monkeys all over the stairs, trying their best to steal food from unsuspecting tourists who were all distracted by taking photos of those same monkeys. I took several photos myself, being very cautious to avoid monkeys on my back as I did.

I bought a packet of biscuits from a vendor and a monkey immediately made a grab for my snack. I gave him a firm "no", and then he started pulling at my clothes in an attempt to convince me to share. In the end, the monkey went away hungry.

Mopping the sweat off my face as I reached the top of the stairs, I descended into the main cave. The morning light shining down in a beam from the opening high above our heads was so beautiful! I can see how the local people could see the light of god(s) in such a divine sight. After taking my fair share of light-filled photos, I bought a ticket for a guided tour of the "dark cave."

The tour was guided to help protect and preserve the cave habitat and inhabitants. We got to hear the squeaky chorus of both insect and fruit bats hanging high above our heads, even though they can't tolerate light and so we couldn't see them. (We got to experience the aroma of guano with our other senses!)

Other cave creatures we encountered included teeny tiny yellow snails, huge creepy long-legged centipedes, big burly cockroaches, and large spindly spiders.

Exhausted from climbing and way too much sunshine, I went back to my hostel to rest before my walking food tour, which was scheduled to start at 5pm. When I arrived in KL the previous night, 5pm was when the thunder, rain, and lightning started. On my third day here, I now realize that you can practically set your clock by the start of the evening storm!

All four of the tour participants still wanted to go even with the weather, so we all set out with umbrellas. We soon learned that umbrellas are no real protection from a monsoon, as the water pounded down from above and splashed up from below, drenching us before we even reached our first destination.

Our tour guide changed plans to an indoor restaurant for our first stop, rather than the food cart he first had in mind. We took shelter from the storm while enjoying sweet creamy tea, spicy rice in banana leaves, and a very tasty soup that we later learned contained sheep's tongue. (Yes, I ate the tongue, and it was great all except the texture.)

When it seemed that the pounding rain was slowing down, we walked on to our next destination. Our guide sat us down and went to get several more dishes for us to try. We each got a leaf and paper-wrapped portion of rice, and there were dishes of beef, chicken, potato cakes, and some fried concoction with anchovies that I just loved.

Next on the tour, we wandered into the farmers market to learn about a variety of unfamiliar produce, and to gaze in horrified fascination at the row of meat stalls.

Then the time came to try the infamous durian fruit – an item so distinctly smelly that it has been banned from many public places. After all the hype, it didn't taste nearly as bad as I expected, and I had no problem taking two bites. We had a lovely rice and sugar confection to remove any lingering unpleasant taste.

The tour continued with "street meat" – a chicken and rice hot dog on a stick, which was one of my favorites of the evening. Next up was a local version of a hamburger, fried with ridiculous amounts of margarine and wrapped in a very thin fried egg. Then was the highlight of the evening... a griddle-fried, banana-filled, sugar-fueled roti (paper-thin pancake).

A very popular street cart serving excellent chicken satay was next on the tour, before our final stop of the evening for blue rice and a noodle dish in fish gravy. After four and a half hours of eating our way through the streets of KL, we finally returned to the hostel, totally stuffed and much better educated about local cuisine... even if I can't remember the names of most of the dishes.

Day 86 - MUD: The Musical
Sunday, June 05, 2016

On my last day in KL, I took in the longest running show in Malaysia, MUD: The Musical. The 60-minute song and dance extravaganza centers around the story of three childhood friends making their way into adulthood during a pivotal time in KL history.

The show begins with the arrival of immigrants to work in the tin mines. It moves forward through time to the official recognition of KL as the capital city, and then to the great fire and subsequent flood that destroyed the city. In the end, the industrious Malaysians rebuilt their city out of bricks formed from the mud leftover from that cataclysmic flood.

The show was well done and the cast was obviously passionate about telling the story. And when audience members were invited up on stage to dance with the cast in their final number... do you even have to wonder if I joined them?

Most of my last two days here have been spent seeking air conditioning and shelter from the sun. The weather report tells me that it's about 93 degrees, but that it feels like 105. The heat is brutal and the intense sunshine feels punishing on top of it. Usually I prefer to walk around to explore a new city, but that just made me sweat buckets so I went underground instead.

Fortunately, KL's subway and train system are very cheap and easy to navigate. I found my way to a few different large air conditioned malls where I could wander in relative comfort. Among those malls was the six-story shopping center at the base of the twin Petronas Towers, filled with glamorous brand name merchandise that I wouldn't dream of buying... even at amazing Malaysian prices!

Yesterday I found a discount outlet mall that was jam packed with locals. The prices were unbeatable (trousers for 30 ringgits/ $7.50 USD), but there was a catch. None of the stores had dressing rooms and none would accept returns.

I ended up buying three items for a total of less than $30, and found that two of them didn't fit right when I finally tried them on back at my accommodation. So... a questionable bargain, but at least I now have one very loose cool dress for comfort in the heat.

I've visited to two American fast food restaurants while in KL. The first was McDonalds, on the advice of my local food tour guide. He told us that we had to try the "Spicy Chicken McDeluxe" which is a dark meat version of the standard sandwich with lots of local spices.

It was indeed tasty, even though definitely identifiable as McDonalds no matter what spices they used. My second visit was to Subway for their Chicken Tandoori sub with sweet chili sauce. Again, it was pretty standard Subway fare, but the sauce certainly did perk it up.

And finally today, I enjoyed a portion of the iconic Malaysian "Chicken Rice." Its pretty much as you'd expect... a small portion of roasted and steamed chicken breast (with skin), over a generous portion of rice cooked in chicken broth, with more savory broth poured over the top.

It was served with sliced cucumber, a very light soup, and sweet chili sauce. The rice was very tasty and the chicken tender. It wasn't significantly different than any other culture's chicken and rice specialty in my experience, but still satisfying.

All in all I've enjoyed my time in KL, but I'm ready to get out of the city and back out into a peaceful natural setting. Fortunately, I'll arrive in Bali tomorrow afternoon and be whisked away to a traditional Lumpung hut overlooking rice fields for the next week!

Day 90 - Hey, Big Spender! (Bali, Indonesia)
Thursday, June 09, 2016

Today is the halfway point in my 180 days of travel, and on this day I'm feeling my wealth and privilege more than most days.

This morning I took a ride at an elephant sanctuary, and as I was sitting on my throne atop the pachyderm, the handler and I had an interesting conversation. I thought it must be a nice job to work with the elephants every day. Although he does love the creatures he works with, his pay equals about $9 USD per day, and he lamented the fact that he can never leave Indonesia to travel earning that kind of money.

I earned the money to fund my travels honestly. I devoted quite a lot of my time and energy to my employer and was fairly compensated for the work I did in that region of the world. I am "entitled" to the relative wealth that I enjoy as a result.

But what truly makes me different from the Indonesian people who are out devoting just as much (if not more) time and energy in the rice fields every day, never to have anything beyond the barest means to support themselves…?

Nothing more than the circumstances of my birth - white, middle class, American, 20th century - dictated my position in life. That's the same story of nearly every human for the last few millennia (at least).

Some are born to privilege and some to poverty. I'm not intrinsically more worthy of wealth and privilege than anyone else, I simply benefit from the luck of the draw when I came into this world, my birth propelling me into far greater opportunity than many others.

The exchange rate between the US dollar and the Indonesian rupiah is ridiculous. I'm taking out half a million in local currency from the ATM almost every day (about $35 USD). I'm tossing around bills with so many zeros on them that it's embarrassing. Every time I take a taxi home after dark I pay 50,000, which seems like it should be a lot, but it converts to less than $4.

I'm contemplating an expensive purchase - at a cost of nearly ten million rupiah. It's something I've wanted for a very long time and the price is actually about half of what I would pay if I made the same purchase at home, even with the high cost of shipping it back.

But again… the emotions I have around this purchase are something like shame and embarrassment. Who can afford to spend that kind of money on something other than a necessity?

In reality, I'm contemplating spending about $1,000 USD for a large heavy steel-pan drum plus shipping. Not an insignificant amount, but affordable given that I'm well under-budget halfway through my trip.

There are those among you who could spend that or more without blinking an eye, and there are those who couldn't even consider spending that amount on anything other than housing, groceries, or strict necessities.

My feelings are compounded by the fact that I have to pay cash for this purchase. It's so easy to hand over my card, or simply enter my digits into a website and click a button. No fuss, no mess, just quick and easy spending without thinking about the amount.

It feels very different when you need to count out ten million in 100,000 unit bills. (I think this is a factor in casinos using chips to gamble instead of cash. You don't have to think about what you're spending!)

I don't have any profound revelations around my feelings about wealth, privilege, and spending. I'm just sharing this with you as I ponder my circumstances and my choices.

Travel does have a way of offering different perspectives...

Day 94 - Peace, Love, and Happines
Monday, June 13, 2016

Here I am on my last day in Bali with another head cold, so I'm taking it easy before shifting into some hardcore travel over the next few days. Travel stresses the body, and I expect that I've encountered viruses that are new to me in each region, and so I've been sick far more often than I've ever been at home... but still, the experience is worth it.

Bali is a lovely, laid back kind of place. The people are warm and friendly, and everybody wants to give me a ride. I walk down the street in town and people immediately offer to be my taxi. A woman on a scooter even stopped on the rural roadside yesterday while I was walking, to ask if I wanted a ride. The economy is depressed (so they're eager to earn some cash), but the people aren't depressed.

The photo above was taken at my accommodation, Capung Sakti, which is owned and run by the Fair Future Foundation. Their mission is to provide free healthcare to the local people. Its funded by the rental house where I'm staying; private tours and transport; and an amazing restaurant in town.

There are three words affixed to the rail of my balcony here: Peace, Love, and Happines. If any of you are pedantic word lovers like I am, you'll notice the misspelling. But here's the thing... perfection isn't required here in Bali. You don't need that extra S to know exactly what that word means.

You don't need to stay within the lines on the road – just avoid obstacles. You don't need exact change – just round a little up or down. You don't need perfect hair or makeup – because the sun and humidity will just melt your attempt at perfection anyway.

Perhaps the key to "happines" lies in forgetting about that extra S. Perhaps peace and love can only exist when we let go of perfection – **let go of the rules that dictate what happines is supposed to look like.**

I'm sick and hot and sweaty, but I'm happi!

134

Day 98 - The Red Center (Alice Springs, Oz)
Friday, June 17, 2016

I arrived in Alice Springs in the "Red Center" of Australia just as the sun was setting on Tuesday night. The world's longest day tour started before sunrise the next day, so I retired early in preparation.

The tour bus picked me up at 5:45am, and so my outback adventure began. Our first stop of the day was for breakfast and a chance to feed emus and kangaroos. I learned that only male emus sit on eggs (how's that for feminism?), and got to meet my first kangaroo in person. They are unbelievably soft, like petting a bunny.

By lunch time our main attraction came into view: the huge red megalith known as Uluru, which is sacred to the Aboriginal people.

Our knowledgeable and entertaining tour guide, Dave, took us on a few walks to see parts of the rock up close, but it was simply too big for us to walk all the way around in our limited 19-hour tour. The tour also made a stop at Kata Tjuta, a collection of more enormous red rock formations in the middle of the flat desert.

Since it's nearly the time of the winter solstice here in Australia, the days are short, as was our time to see all of the sites. We rushed to get back to the Uluru viewing point so that we could witness the magic of the sunset light changing the rock into shades of purple and silver. While we waited for the sun to move to the horizon, our guides cooked up a feast in the parking lot – including very tasty kangaroo steaks!

With unlimited wine, beer, and champagne flowing freely, my fellow passengers and I milled about chatting with each other in the last few minutes of daylight. And then... the rain started to fall. There would be no sunset color changes for us that night, but we did get to see a rainbow over Uluru as the storm cleared away while dinner started.

After the long journey back, I arrived at my accommodation around 12:45am. I took it easy the next day, wandering all around the small town of Alice Springs.

I enjoyed the reptile center (complete with large crocodile, thorny devils, and several deadly snakes), and many opportunities to view Aboriginal artwork. In the evening I went to the hottest pub in town, enjoying a pint and a pizza under the stars with the locals having a good time all around me.

On my final day in Alice, I visited the highly recommended Desert Park to see more local flora and fauna. I got to spend more  time up close and personal with kangaroos, including this alpha male who was lounging in the sun as if he was posing for a centerfold. Another highlight of the park was the free flying bird show, with falcons, owls, and eagles swooping in out of the sky on cue.

This whole time I've been observing that winter in the center of Oz is warmer and sunnier than most summer days in my home of Seattle. (I wouldn't want to be here roasting in summer!) But this afternoon, my faith in the Australian winter was restored with a hailstorm of epic proportions.

I was lounging in my sundress in the backyard of the hostel when the thunder started rolling and the dark clouds started filling up the sky. It was only moments before the first few drops of rain fell and I moved inside. In less than a minute, the rain turned to hail, and before long the backyard was invisible.

The paved pathway turned into a river, and the lawn turned into a swamp. The sun shades were bowed under the weight of of ice pellets. The noise on the tin roof of my little hut was deafening. Then the storm passed, and my fellow guests at the hostel ran outside to have hail-ball fights and take pictures of the stunningly changed landscape.

Tomorrow I begin a long bus journey south. I can expect seemingly endless stretches of desert with the occasional roadhouse every few hundred kilometers. Off on another adventure!

Day 100 - Treasure Hunt (Coober Pedy, Oz)
Sunday, June 19, 2016

The desert town of Alice Springs still had icy piles of hail the morning after that epic storm. Businesses were still cleaning up from flooding and downed trees branches were everywhere. I saw a kayaker floating down the Todd River, which had been dry the day before. One storm can sure change the landscape!

And with that, my bus departed into the wide open desert. Eight hours and one glorious deep red sunset later, we arrived in the tiny opal mining town of Coober Pedy.

I checked into my cozy cave motel and spent my first ever night underground. The sleep was dark, warm, and peaceful. Maybe our cave dwelling ancestors knew a good thing when they found it!

In the morning I set out to explore the town. My first stop was the Catacomb Church – an underground cave of Anglican worship – where I found the Sunday service just about to start. I took the opportunity to sit in for the beginning of the service, complete with Aussie-centric songs praising the creation of local natural wonders. The local congregation seemed to be about a dozen people, with more guests in attendance than regulars.

As an acknowledged tourist, I only stayed for part of the service and then quietly continued on with my wanderings. Thus began my day of checking out almost every tourist site, and every single opal shop in town.

There are twenty or so shops, all selling a variety of opal jewelry and loose stones, Aboriginal artwork, boomerangs and didgeridoos. I ducked and squeezed my way through a real sandstone opal mine, and tried (unsuccessfully, again) to make a pleasing sound out of a didgeridoo. I even toured a real dugout (underground cave) home.

I LOVE rocks and gemstones. I have a moderate collection at home and have a hard time resisting all of those shiny pretty things, but opals come with hefty price tags - even when they're direct from the source here at the mines.

So I took my time perusing every stone in every shop. I went back to a few shops more than once, until I finally narrowed down two shops that had the polished egg-shape that I was looking for. It turns out that those two shops were owned by a married couple, and he was willing to make me a deal on the stone I wanted in her shop... when she didn't want to offer a discount!

With hopes that I didn't cause any marital strife, I pocketed my treasure and trudged back to my motel after a long day of hunting. The motel manager drove me down to the local roadhouse to await my overnight bus ride, about three hours later.

I now sit in the roadhouse (one of only two restaurants in this town), enjoying the free wifi and a glass of Australian shiraz. I have an 11-hour ride to look forward to this evening. I suspect this first glass of wine won't be my last, with two more hours to go before departure.

The moon is nearly full tonight and I'm told that makes the kangaroos come out to play on the highway. All of the busses here have large wildlife-repelling grills in front, due to the frequent instances of animals appearing on the roadway without warning.

With this overnight drive, there's a very good chance that a suicidal kangaroo may decide to throw himself in front of our bus, so I'll be sure to wear my seatbelt!

Day 103 - Barossa Buzz (Adelaide, Australia)
Wednesday, June 22, 2016

The South Australian region of the Barossa Valley is famous for its vineyards, most notably of the Shiraz variety (my favorite!) Today I took an all-day wine tasting tour in the Valley, including four separate wineries and so many different wines that I lost count. That glow you see in my cheeks isn't just from the wind!

My favorite stop of the day was the Peter Lehmann Winery, named after the man whose vision, courage, and integrity saved the Barossa Valley wine industry at a critical point. Not only did I get to enjoy many fine wines, but I got the bonus inspiration of hearing a man's life story that was well worth the telling.

At a time when the local grape growing industry was about to collapse due to overproduction, Lehmann took a huge gamble and began his own winery. Growers provided him with fruit for no cost other than his promise that he would pay them as soon as the wine turned a profit – which is exactly what he did.

Without his bold actions, those growers and countless families would have lost their livelihood and Australia wouldn't be the top producer of Shiraz in the world today.

Another stop along the tour included a visit to the oldest Shiraz grapevines in the world, at the ripe old age (I couldn't resist the pun) of 173 years. The secret to their long life appears to be stress! Being in such a dry region, the vines are forced to grow very deep roots in search of water, and so produce very small fruits that are intensely flavored. Grapes grown in wetter regions are much larger and juicier, but without nearly the same richness of flavor.

In addition to wine tasting, I've been enjoying the exceptionally well organized city of Adelaide, where I'm staying in South Australia. This is a planned city and it shows. Gardens are plentiful, streets are easy to navigate, and there's a sense of calm that's unusual for a city this size.

On my first day in town, I took a stroll through the Botanical Gardens, including a stunning pyramid-like greenhouse that contains local and exotic foliage. The greenhouse features one of the infamous corpse flower plants - known for blooming only once every seven years, at which point it smells like decaying flesh. Thankfully, it wasn't in bloom for my visit!

With so much plant life, the wildlife in the Botanical Gardens is abundant as well. There are many species of birds, and I stopped at one point to witness something I've never seen before. First I noticed the sound of loud chatter up in the red gum trees. Then I noticed that the very large birds high in the branches appeared to be... upside down.

Of course, those weren't birds at all, but hundreds of giant fruit bats! I watched in fascination as many of them flapped their scal-loped-edged wings as they hung from their talons. I was awed when one would loosen his grip, spread his wings, and soar through the air to another perch.

Its winter here in Australia and the weather has been a bit damp and chilly. I took shelter from the rain yesterday and indulged my inner geek by going to a matinee of the new X-Men movie. The weather doesn't usually stop me from exploring, but travel is now my full time job and even adventurers need a day off every now and then.

Day 106 - Campfire in the City (Melbourne, Oz)
Saturday, June 25, 2016

In the Melbourne central business district, a campfire is burning. In the shadow of skyscrapers and cathedral spires, next to the noise of tram lines and traffic, a perpetual flame is kept burning throughout winter.

The sign says that this fire is a gift from the Aboriginal people, warmly welcoming visitors to their land as part of the city's Light in Winter festival. Stone benches surround the large sandy fire pit, with cushions to separate warm behinds from the cold sur-face. Locals and tourists alike gather around to bask in the red glow of the fire, and on some nights (so the sign tells me), there is storytelling.

I've been feeling like I'm walking around in an alternate reality. Most of what I've experienced of Melbourne so far has been very Western. Lots of restaurants, lots of shopping, lots of big tall office buildings, lots of people walking briskly about their business. It could be any large American city and I'd never know the difference... except for the odd sensation of time displacement.

I'm now fifteen hours ahead of my home time zone. When I phone home, my call usually reaches its destination the day before I placed it.

Last weekend I phoned in to join a family party that was on a Saturday afternoon, but I had to get up early on Sunday morning to make the call. When I post with friends on facebook, most of them are on a vastly different schedule than me. So while my surroundings look much like home (complete with gray skies and rain), I keep getting reminders that I'm very far away.

It didn't feel so odd when I was in obviously foreign countries where the language and culture were unfamiliar to me and the people looked very different from me. In those places it was easy to roll with the differences, comfortably aware of my foreign environment. Here, I'm unconsciously lulled into a false sense of home, only to be jarred back to the (alternate) reality of a faraway land by little things.

Stumbling upon that campfire delighted me. Although I've been in many cities by this time, no other city cared to build a socially-oriented fire in the middle of the hustle and bustle. That campfire is uniquely Melbourne (as far as I know), and it helped to ground me in the true reality of this slice of Australian culture.

I sat there on my padded bench gazing up at the tall city buildings, watching the traffic go by, hearing the thumping bass of a nearby night club. I stared into the dancing flames and let my vision go blurry, safe in the knowledge that – even in the middle of this urban atmosphere where I should always be on my guard – I could take that moment to open to the circle around me.

With more than three weeks still to go in Australia, I'll try to be more vigilant in looking for the unique quirks of each place. It's too easy to be complacent and fall into thinking a new place is just like home, without going deeper into its identity.

Australia isn't an alternate reality to the USA or other Western locations, it is its own beautiful land with its own personality. I'm pleased to make your acquaintance, Oz!

Day 107 - Jazz of Remembrance
Sunday, June 26, 2016

I spent my last day in Melbourne exploring the Royal Botanic Garden. I wandered my way to the Shrine of Remembrance located in the Garden, which was built to honor the many Australians who lost their lives fighting in World War I. I found myself just in time for a free concert offered by the Air Force Jazz Band entitled: Jazz of Remembrance.

I was raised on American jazz and expected to hear a lot of familiar classics. However, I wasn't aware that the art form of jazz had inspired other nations, and was surprised to find this concert centered around French composers in honor of the French soil where so many of the battles were fought.

The music was deeply emotionally evocative, and while I definitely recognized the style as jazz, the mood was far different than the classics I grew up with. The band did an excellent job of not only performing beautiful music, but also using their talents to artfully represent the grief and loss that the Australian people suffered as their loved ones died and were buried so far from home.

Day 109 - A Relative Unknown (Tasmania, Oz)
Tuesday, June 28, 2016

My first full day on the island south of the Australian mainland known as Tasmania, I got a private guided tour from my cousin Judy, whom I never met before this morning.

My paternal grandmother was born into a large family in Australia, but I've never had the chance to meet most of those descendants so it was an absolute pleasure getting to know this not-so-distant relative.

We look so happy because we just escaped from Richmond Gaol, Australia's oldest prison still standing. (Not still full of prisoners, thankfully, but the building still exists.)

In the 1800s that prison was filled with transported convicts with crimes ranging from forgery to murder. We also viewed the women's solitary confinement room, where the offense of "insolence" was punished by spending days in the dark cramped quarters with no furnishings except a small bucket for a toilet.

After touring the gaol, we walked along the nearby river, even catching a glimpse of a pair of black swans. We saw a beautifully arched bridge – built by convicts, of course. (They already built their own prison, why not a bridge for the town as well?) We strolled the streets of the small town of Richmond, found some of Judy's husband's drawings for sale in a local shop, and stopped for a cup of tea with lunch.

All the while I was entertained with stories of family whom I never had the chance to know, and comparisons with family traits that we both share. (I'm not the only one who prefers a colder climate, nor the only one who has suffered heat exhaustion.) We caught up on news of my immediate family and enjoyed finding similarities in our sometimes quirky senses of humor.

We had a great time at our next stop, throwing food pellets into trout-filled ponds and watching the huge fat fish jump all over each other to get some. I couldn't help giggling every time Judy ironically shouted out "holy mackerel!" in surprise at the trouts' antics.

We hunted for the elusive platypus, which we were told lives in the trout pond, but sadly the mysterious mammal chose not to make an appearance. Finishing up the day with a cuppa tea and a slice of beetroot chocolate cake (so delicious!), Judy then returned me to my hostel.

I look forward to returning the favor with a tour around the Pacific Northwest when she gets the chance to visit!

Day 112 - Woods and Whiskies
Friday, July 01, 2016

Woods and whiskies – two of my favorite things, all in one day!

Yesterday I took the free shuttle offered by my hostel to the top of Mount Wellington. It was a gorgeous drive up to the top of the cloud-shrouded peak, where visibility was only about twenty feet.

The air was damp and chilled, and the winter wind cut through my clothing as if I was wearing nothing at all. Considering that there was no view through the dense cloud anyway, and that hypothermia was a very real possibility, I didn't mind letting the 20-somethings on the shuttle jump out to have their adventure from the top, while I asked the driver to drop me off a little further down the mountain.

About halfway back down to the base of the mountain, I left the van to trek down some of the many trails winding around Mt. Wellie, as the locals call it. (Many words in Oz are shortened to an "ie" at the end – brekkie for breakfast, Tassie for Tasmania, Brizzie for Brisbane, etc.)

The trail was rugged and rocky, while covered with a thick layer of decaying leaves. The going was a bit rough and slippery, but then the forest offered up a walking stick of dead wood of just the right size for me, which saved me from falling at least a few times.

The mountain is covered in trees and alive with the usual woodland wildlife. The wind that was so cutting on the top of the peak was much gentler when filtered through the tall trees. Several times I stood completely still and silent, just to enjoy the music of the trees rustling softly in the breeze. I tried to capture that lovely serenity in memory, to sustain my inner peace as I enter the chaotic noise of the city of Sydney tomorrow.

I hiked to the base of the mountain within an hour, detouring to trek by the beautiful Silver Falls along the way. Since this is a civilized country, there was a pub with a roaring fire waiting at the base, where mulled cider was ready to thaw out chilled trekkers.

I warmed up and returned to town, then wandered to the only maker of whisky in all of Tasmania – the Lark Distillery. The tasting sampler consisted of three selections: the single malt 43%, the single malt cask strength 58%, and the whisky liqueur.

Starting with the 43% as recommended, I inhaled the scent of the heady brew and my eyes rolled back with pleasure. The first small sip caressed my tongue and became nothing more than vapor in my mouth, the taste lingering long after the liquid evaporated.

The second, slightly larger sip actually made it down my throat, and planted a lovely seed of warmth deep in my belly. I continued sniffing and sipping until the "half measure" portion was all gone, and I was eager to try the next elixir.

Next was the 58% cask strength. I was nearly drunk just from inhaling the fumes of that one, but I wanted the taste experience as well. My eyes watered with the potency of the drink, but the taste was so full and rich that I continued sipping anyway. After a few sips, I cut it with a splash of water, making the rest of it much easier to consume.

The third and final sample was the whisky liqueur, formally titled "Slainte'". The aroma of this one was fruity and sweet and complex, and I sat there just sniffing it for several minutes.

It smelled so good that I almost didn't want to taste it for fear that it couldn't possibly live up to the expectation set by the scent, but when I finally did take that first sip… it was like a kiss of golden sunshine that had passed through honeyed nectar in a summer meadow.

Words can't even begin to describe the incredible flavor of that whisky liqueur, and the distillery isn't allowed to export out of Australia, so y'all are just going to have to visit Tasmania yourselves to form your own opinion!

Day 114 - Night on the Town (Sydney, Oz)
Sunday, July 03, 2016

I thought that the best way to see the famous Sydney Opera House would be to attend an actual opera, so I chose what looked like a very interesting selection from their list of events. Then I decided to make a night of it, getting dressed up and taking myself out for a nice meal before the show.

I enjoyed a lovely dinner of grilled kangaroo steak and a glass of Australian shiraz in celebration of my solo date night. I ate at an outdoor bistro overlooking Sydney Harbour, the Harbour Bridge, and all of the many passersby wandering the pier on a Saturday night. Even though we're in the heart of winter here in Sydney, the weather has been very mild (low 60s F during the day) and the restaurant had large patio heaters so it was very comfortable.

The show I chose was called The Love of Three Oranges and was meant to be something of a fairytale farce, which is unusual for the genre of opera. I appreciate random, weird, fantastical sorts of things, so that sounded right up my alley.

I arrived at the theatre early to enjoy another glass of wine while mingling with all of the other theatre-goers doing the same thing, and gazing up at the fascinating architecture of the opera house.

When the time came, I took my reserved seat and settled in with anticipation of enjoyable entertainment. The show started promisingly, with a great orchestra in the pit and a prologue of "The Ridiculous" (the name for the chorus) arguing in song over whether a comedy or a tragedy should be performed.

I've liked opera since I was a teenager. I'm familiar with the usual composition of aria (a standalone melody), chorus (everybody on stage singing together), and recitative (less melodic, basically used for singing dialogue).

I understood going in that this was an opera that makes fun of opera. Great! But here's the thing... the ENTIRE opera was done in recitative style. It reminded me of an exercise we did in my college drama class where we would act out a scene in a particular style. When we did "opera style", our dialogue took the form of sustained high notes and plunging low notes, the repetitive peaks and valleys so overly dramatized that it was hard to listen to for very long.

I really tried to like the show. I have no complaints about the orchestra or the instrumental score, but the libretto... the "melody" and lyrics... became like fingernails on a chalkboard to me by the third act.

It offended my musical sensibilities, with no rhythm or recognizable musical patterns at all. I felt pity for the singers, wondering if they could possibly have any enjoyment or satisfaction in performing that – and wondering how they ever managed to commit such a bizarre string of notes to memory.

There was something of a plot, but the events and characters were so superficial, random, and weird (again, I usually like random and weird), that there was no chance for the audience to become invested in the story. There were several weak puns, but nothing actually clever.

I tried to care whether or not the Prince got to live happily ever after with his beloved third orange, but I was honestly just longing for the pain of the music to end.

What more can I say? The costumes were elaborate and colorful. There were some interesting dance sequences with people dressed as playing cards and saguaro cactuses. The large abstract oranges, which each opened to reveal a princess, were beautiful.

I'm still glad that I got to see a show at the Sydney Opera House, and this one was definitely memorable. Had I just seen a standard opera, no matter how enjoyable, I probably would have forgotten it in time.

This experience is now seared into my memory like the painful burn of a juicy orange squirted directly into my eye. I won't be forgetting that any time soon!

Day 120 – Bellbunya (Eumundi, Australia)
Friday, July 08, 2016

After three weeks of travel through Australia, moving every few days to a new location, I am now temporarily settled in the community of Bellbunya near the Sunshine Coast.

I was a little tired of playing tourist - being herded around with hordes of other foreigners through notable sites, staying in hostels with low sleep quality, and spending too much time in cities. It was fun for a while, but I was longing for something more productive to do with my time, and to make deeper connections with the people around me.

My longing is being fulfilled here in community again! There are about a dozen full time community members living here, as well as a handful of people like me who are here for anywhere from a couple of weeks to a few months, some of whom are considering staying on longer term.

The flow of this community is more free-form than I've experienced before. Volunteers like myself are expected to work eighteen hours per week, but how and when we contribute is entirely up to us.

There is no set structure for each day, no daily meetings other than dinner, and no expectation to work at anything that doesn't inspire or appeal to each individual. It can be a little challenging to show up and just start pitching in with very little knowledge of how things work around here, but I've found that whatever I do is appreciated.

My first day I looked at the "to be done" board and saw a lot of gardening chores that I wouldn't know where to start with, a few random fixes needed, and one request to organize the shared office space.

Organize? Score! Now there's something I'm good at. So after asking a few questions to assure that I didn't step on anyone's toes or screw up anything too badly, I got to work and put in three hours for the day. The office, where I'm typing this very blog, feels a lot better now.

The next day I asked around to see who needed assistance. I ended up helping to feed the chickens and ducks, as well as spreading compost and collecting eggs. I did some organizing of the large linen closet, and helped in the kitchen to cater lunch and dinner for a group of two dozen student volunteers.

In between my few hours of work each day, I have lots of time to connect with the amazing members and guests of the community. I love hearing about others' travels, adventures, and challenges as they each live their own unique lives, seeking meaning and fulfillment in so many different ways.

The property of Bellbunya itself is also amazingly beautiful. Our meals include lots of fruit and vegetables fresh out of the garden, including bananas - assuming the wild turkeys haven't eaten them all!

Even though we aren't far away from a town, the night sky is dark enough to showcase an incredible number of stars. Last night we enjoyed an outdoor fire, sitting under that endless black sky twinkling with little stars. That was another one of those moments that I captured for my memory - the comforting heat of the fire in front of me, the peaceful dark of the sky above me, and the friendly camaraderie of beautiful people around me.

Day 124 - A Different Pace
Wednesday, July 13, 2016

Having spent just over a week at the Bellbunya community now, I'm really enjoying the more relaxed pace of life around here. Things get done, but there's no rush and no pushing.

I still wake up fairly early (6:00-6:30am), so I guess that the verdict is that I'm truly a morning person now. I enjoy a gentle morning, first making a cup of tea in the shared kitchen, with breakfast sometime after that. By 9am, I'm usually looking for some tasks so that I can put in my average of three hours work for the day.

Yesterday I took the day off with a couple others to learn a basic style of leather shoemaking from one of the full time residents. The four of us shared a lovely day of crafting and friendship.

Today I pitched in with a local volunteer commitment that Bellbunya makes twice weekly to the nearby town of Eumundi. Although Eumundi is a very small town on its own (one main street with a handful of shops, restaurants, and pubs), it hosts a large open-air public market twice every week. The Eumundi Market is many times the size of most weekly farmers' markets I've visited, and very well attended by people from outlying towns and even international visitors.

My job for today was to manage one of the large parking lots that support the market, wearing a reflective vest and carrying a flag to direct the cars into neat rows as market patrons began arriving. It was a pleasant work shift, even though arrivals were coming in at a quick pace for the first couple of hours. I even ended up helping direct road traffic for a while, which was backed up to the intersection with vehicles waiting to turn into the busy parking lots.

With my hourly commitment for the day done, I now have the afternoon free to read a book and write my blog. I may wander through the woods or take a walk down the road to the one very small shop within walking distance. I'd like to take a shower, but I recently met a creature in there that makes me want to avoid the bathroom altogether.

As I'm enjoying this pace with plenty of time to breathe and rest and think, I let my thoughts drift back to my previous lifestyle. I used to wake up to an alarm before I was fully rested, and jump quickly into a fast-paced morning that required all of my attention and energy.

My nine or ten hour workday used to progress at a brisk pace, only to continue with more chores after I got home. I used to collapse in the evening, too exhausted to be social or creative - with just enough energy remaining to bond with my sofa and television before beginning the whole cycle again the next day.

That fast-paced lifestyle just doesn't suit me anymore. I'm not ready for retirement yet, of course, but I'm definitely ready to adopt a more reasonable and healthy long term pace to my life than the corporate desk job schedule allows.

I smile more and scowl less now. I don't get angry and frustrated on a regular basis like I used to, because I'm not always running on empty. My mood is more stable and I can more accurately understand my natural range of emotions because I'm not constantly reacting from a state of overwhelming stress.

I don't know how yet, but I feel like I want to make this part of my life's work - helping to rescue others from the destructive consequences of an over-stressed life, and move into a healthier, happier existence (whatever that may look like for each individual).

I want to help others "retreat forward" into relaxed productivity and holistic self awareness. The question is how to make that a reality...

Day 130 - Social vs. Solitude
Tuesday, July 19, 2016

My life is designed so that I can enjoy the large amounts of solitude that I need to maintain my emotional balance. While I love people and treasure my relationships, I also recognize that spending significant time on my own is necessary for recharging my vital energies.

Over the last two weeks I had the privilege and pleasure of forming deep heart connections with many members of the Bellbunya community. It felt so good to develop and nurture those relationships that I neglected my usual need for solitude.

In addition, I chose to stay in a dorm rather than request my own room, so even my unconscious hours were spent with company. I didn't realize how depleted my social stamina had become until the community hosted a large party over the weekend. One of the core members of the community had a milestone birthday, and so lots of guests converged on the property for the festivities.

Every guest that I met or spoke to was a lovely and fascinating person. Strangers greeted me with hugs and kisses, and we delved into deep topics within minutes of our introductions. But even in the first hour of the gathering, I felt the urge to run and hide from the small crowd.

I forced myself to stay for a while, feeling both the desire to honor the birthday girl and an obligation to make merry with new friends. And yet, I kept finding excuses to leave the party and go off to tend a fire or clean up dishes. I eventually did rejoin the party once the dinner bell sounded (food is a powerful motivator), but still had some sense of being a trapped animal in the over-crowded space.

Thinking back on my cruise across the Atlantic earlier in my journey, I reflected on the two social extremes.

On the ship, I was starved for heartfelt social interaction. I was bored and restless and had far more solitude than I needed. At Bellbunya, I have a wealth of deep connections with amazing people, but no time on my own to rest and recharge from all that social stimulation.

Community offers so many opportunities to stretch, grow, and test our personal boundaries. It also provides an atmosphere in which to find the limits that we absolutely must respect within ourselves to maintain our own health and happiness. I've now established some of my own limits based on my experiences with these communities.

I still have more limits to test and discover, but I feel stronger and more stable from having gained this deeper self-knowledge.

Having a more solid idea of what I need to maintain my personal balance helps me to set firm boundaries in the future, so that I can meet my own needs and be more present to experience all of the elements of my life... without the urge to escape.

Day 135 - Having Fun (Brisbane & Auckland)
Sunday, July 24, 2016

After leaving the community of Bellbunya, I spent one day in the city of Brisbane before traveling on to New Zealand. I wasn't interested in playing tourist in the city, but I did find a production of "We Will Rock You", a musical inspired by the well-known songs of the epic rock band Queen. I bought myself a matinee ticket in the second balcony, where I had the luxury of the whole section to myself.

The show did not disappoint! The plot had a sci-fi vibe to it, being set in a dystopian future where any music that wasn't generated by the ruling corporation was outlawed. Of course, this spawned a rebel class of Bohemians in search of their Rhapsody, even though they had no real understanding of exactly what rock and roll could be.

Galileo Figaro was the hero of the story, going on a journey of personal discovery with his lady love, Scaramoosh, leading to the climax featuring the iconic number, "We Are the Champions."

The script was rich with jokes pulled from song lyrics and pop culture. It was a rocking good time with the audience singing, clapping, stomping, and waving their arms in the air. I left the theater feeling totally energized and ready to take on the world!

The next day I departed for Auckland, and made it to our B&B. My sister Susie and I enjoyed our reunion a couple of hours later when she arrived from Sydney that same night.

Our next day was spent exploring the city of Auckland. The first stop was a place called Odyssey Sensory Maze. The place may have been designed for kids, but we had so much fun!

The entrance was a dark tunnel leading over a bridge that vibrated under our feet. We pushed on through the next doorway, leading us into a room with several scent-boxes, where we got to test our senses of smell. Another room had mirrors on the floor and ceiling with laser lights creating an effect similar to the streaming green data in The Matrix. Susie dropped to the floor and began "swimming in space", appearing to float between the mirrored surfaces and the lasers.

The following day, we returned to downtown Auckland and made our way to the waterfront, where we caught a ferry across the harbor to the small town of Devonport. We wandered the town, found some lunch, and climbed to the highest point to enjoy spectacular views. The wind was strong and we had fun taking action photos.

Day 138 BlackWater Rafting (Waitomo Caves)
Wednesday, July 27, 2016

Today my sister and I embarked on a new adventure for both of us – black water rafting. In other words, white water rafting in the total darkness of an underground river.

After gearing up in cold, clammy wet suits (including booties, boots, and helmets with lights) our group was taken to a river near one of the entrances to the Waitomo Caves on the North Island of New Zealand.

The practice challenge was jumping from four feet high into a slow moving above-ground river - backwards. The jump position was rear end inserted into the center of an inner tube, as shown in this flattering photo. (Hey, let's see *you* try to look cute while jumping into a freezing river!)

The water was... refreshing, or at least it might have been in summer. It's winter here in the southern hemisphere and that river was ice cold, but the wetsuits made the chilly water bearable.

Next we entered the cave through a narrow gap in the rocks, stepping carefully into the fast flowing water due to recent rainstorms. Once our whole group was in the cave, we set off walking through the shallow underground river carrying our tubes, with the rough limestone walls creating some very slim passages.

Continuing on, we scrambled over underwater rocks and bumped our helmets on ceilings with a clearance height of only twelve inches from the surface of the water in some places. A few times we came upon water deep enough that we had to mount our inner tubes in the rear-in-hole position and let the river carry us downstream. In some areas we formed a chain of inner tubes, each person grabbing the feet of the person behind them.

The biggest challenge of the day was repeating that backward jump maneuver over a short, but raging waterfall in the depths of the cave. Our guides gave no opportunity for reluctance or second thoughts, almost pushing us each off the ledge as our turn to jump approached. We all made the leap successfully and without hesitation.

At one point in the tour, I found myself at the front of the line for the next float down the swollen underground river. I positioned myself in my tube as the guide instructed, and started scooting my way across the rock and into deeper water.

That's when my body caught the current – but my inner tube slipped out from under me. I was fully immersed in the dark river, had no idea what was coming next, and had no idea how to get myself back onto the inner tube that I was still clinging to for dear life.

One plaintive "help?" escaped my lips before I noticed the light of another guide only a few meters away, and noticed her outstretched hand to catch me before I was swept blindly around the bend.

I was concerned that Susie might have been worried by my cry for help as I disappeared into the darkness, but instead... she moved back in the line and waited for the guide to work out a safer path for the next person to take. (Ha!) Our group reunited without further incident after my little misadventure and we continued onward.

The absolute best part of the tour was when we were in our tubes floating down a slower part of the river with our head lamps off. We were in total darkness, except for the galaxy of tiny luminescent blue dots of the glow worms hanging from the ceiling of the cave high above us. The sound of the roaring water had died down, and we simply rode the current in peaceful silence under the subtle glow above us.

And in the end, I saw a literal light at the end of the tunnel. At first it was just a sliver in the darkness, and then it grew into a wide opening in the rock framing the spectacular lush greenery of the rain forest. We had so much fun, but were tired and ready to be done with excitement by that point. That light meant warmth and dryness ahead!

Day 144 - Te Papa (Wellington, New Zealand)
Tuesday, August 02, 2016

Everybody says that the "must visit" spot in Wellington is the Te Papa Museum, and I have to agree after spending most of today enjoying it! First things first, apparently **all** museums in New Zealand have free entry. (Has anybody mentioned that idea to Europe?) Second, the place is chock full of interesting and interactive exhibits over six floors.

I started from the ground up and visited the "Blood Earth Fire" section first. This exhibit explored the layers that make up our planet from core to crust. It included chunks of minerals like granite and iron for visitors to pick up and compare weights, to better understand the composition of our Earth.

Continuing the theme of the natural world, the exhibits transitioned into native animals – past and present. Fossils and dinosaur bones led to taxidermied beasts and a pygmy blue whale skeleton suspended from the rafters. Further on I found the only Colossal Squid on display in the entire world, next to a 3-D film recreation of how that ginormous squid was accidentally caught by a research vessel.

Up the stairs, exhibits moved from nature to culture. I enjoyed a film profiling several New Zealanders (also known as Kiwis) and their varied lifestyles – a nature photographer living in solitude, a beat-boxing city courier, and a living-off-the-land homesteader among others.

Video kiosks showed interviews with Kiwis who had fought against apartheid and for civil rights. Exhibits explored music, fashions, fads, and more of the Kiwi people.

Moving higher up into the museum, I found the floor dedicated to the native Maori people and their culture. Displays showcased the weapons, tools, clothing, and tattoos of the Maori.

My favorite part was a film that depicted the story behind a famous Haka (a traditional warriors' show of strength and intimidation). I could definitely imagine how the testosterone-charged display of stomping, thigh smacking, chest-beating, tongue wagging, eye bulging, shouting, and sharp movements would intimidate any potential challengers!

The next floor of the museum was dedicated to more recent cultrual phenomena like fridge poetry, mobile phone selfies, and modern art. The highest floors were devoted to painting, pottery, and sculptures.

And on top of all that amazing history, knowledge, and culture...

the place had free wifi and multiple cafes on site. The architecture of the building was beautiful, and the staff were friendly and helpful. I didn't mean to write an entire blog as an advertisement for Te Papa, but the rumors are true! When in Wellington, make sure that you visit, too.

Day 147 - Reflections on Men
Friday, August 05, 2016

This photo was taken at the Te Papa Museum in Wellington. Not only did it make me giggle, but it got me thinking. I haven't really written anything about my encounters with men along my journey, but they're part of my overall experience so I'll correct that oversight now.

I'm single, which has been true for most of my life. When I was younger, I embraced vacation romance with vigor. It seemed that every time I traveled I would have some whirlwind love story, which I would then try to translate into a long term relationship once I returned home (despite the distance). Those relationships inevitably ended after a short time.

I went through that cycle a few times before I accepted that relationships take time and proximity to develop, and I gave up the idea of maintaining any long distance love connection. So when I started this journey, romance wasn't on my mind. However, that doesn't mean that the men of the world had similarly platonic intentions toward me.

A couple of months into my journey, I met a man staying at the same accommodation as me. I wandered through his outdoor birthday party, where he used cake and whiskey to lure me into staying. He immediately began trying to put the moves on me, and I immediately started saying no. But the alcohol and sugar had me smiling and laughing (and probably sending mixed signals), and his pursuit continued.

I was flattered by the attention and honestly enjoyed his company, but was also really uncomfortable with his persistence after my repeated "no" for an answer. After I continued on with my journey, I decided that I need to be more forceful with my personal boundaries in the future, and I got the opportunity to practice again not long after that.

Upon discovering a drum circle in Athens one evening, I sat down to enjoy the music. One of the drummers attempted to lay claim to me, putting his arm around me and proclaiming me his princess. (gag!) I clearly told him that his touching made me uncomfortable, which reduced his affections somewhat, but he continued trying to woo me.

Before long, I realized that he also wouldn't accept "no" for an answer. As the sun was going down, I said goodbye without excuse and just kept walking away despite his cries of, "hey baby...?" I felt good that I remained strong in my boundaries.

A few countries later, I finally got to enjoy a mutual interest. Through random chance, I found myself having a long conversation with a man next to me on a lengthy bus ride. We were both surprised to find that we shared startlingly similar values, philosophies, and personal goals.

Dedication to his work prevented him from following through on his request to meet me for drinks before I left town, but before that encounter I had no idea that the ability to make good life choices could be so sexy in man. At least I learned something!

Not long after that, I met a man who instantly caught my eye with his good looks. I tried to ignore the immediate physical attraction as shallow, but then he showed himself to be just as beautiful on the inside. We shared interests, values, laughter and hugs... which set off a crush of such intensity in me that I hadn't experienced since my teen years!

Despite the unusual intensity of emotion that I was feeling, my practical side clearly recognized that our two life paths were only intersecting for a very short time. Even if the interest was mutual, there was no real opportunity for us to explore that connection in any depth.

And so I made my inner starry-eyed teenager sit in the corner and pout, while my outer mature woman enjoyed a satisfying (albeit brief) platonic friendship with the beautiful man.

With each of these encounters with men along the way, I've reflected on my past relationships. I think about how I could have held stronger boundaries, and how I could have made my own needs better known. I think about how important shared values are to me, and how easily I've dismissed them in the past. I think about how intensity of emotion and depth of emotion aren't always the same thing.

So I learn and I grow and I hope that these experiences help me continue making good choices in the future. I look forward to connecting with a man again someday... when I can stick around for a while!

Day 150 - Temporal Dynamics (TransPacific)
Tuesday, August 09, 2016

Holy flux capacitor, I'm traveling back in time! In the wee hours of Wednesday morning I'll depart New Zealand and then arrive in Hawaii on Tuesday morning. This is made possible by passing through the strange and unnatural construct known as the International Date Line.

The equator is an imaginary line around the latitudinal center of

164

our planet, and although there's no visible indication as I discovered on my cruise, at least the lack of seasonal shifts along that line offers some physical evidence to support it's existence. By comparison, the Date Line is a work of pure fiction. There's no physical characteristic on this planet that defines one calendar date from another.

Today is Tuesday and I'll check out of my New Zealand hotel at 11:30am. Tomorrow will also be Tuesday when I arrive in Hawaii at 11:00am. (At least I'm not repeating a Monday, right?) I won't actually be a day younger, nor will the rotation of the world be reversed while I'm flying across the Pacific Ocean. And yet... I'm going to live the same date twice.

One of those mysterious things about going around in a circle is that eventually you go so far forward that you end up going backward. With each time zone I've crossed over the last five months of eastward travel around the globe, I've saved up a balance of hours that is now coming due. My frequent flyer miles have earned me one bonus day on this planet... at least according to an imaginary construct!

Day 155 - Au Naturel (Big Island of Hawaii)
Friday, August 12, 2016

Here I am in Hawaii, in a tiny off-grid cabin on three private jungle-covered acres of land. Both the shower and the toilet are outside of the cabin. The dining lanai is also outside, under cover, supported by beautiful natural mango wood trunks. And being Hawaii, the weather is gloriously soft and warm at all hours of the day and night. Even the daily rain is soft and warm!

This might be 'too much information' for some of you, but I have to say that the absolute best thing about being out here is being naked in nature. It's so warm that clothes are unnecessary and so private (a locked gate at the end of the long driveway) that I have no worries of unexpected visitors. It's sheer pleasure to feel the Hawaiian air on every inch my skin!

But of course, humans aren't the only creatures that love this atmosphere. I'm sharing the cabin with lots of cute little green geckos and a horde of tiny ants that congregate in the kitchen sink.

When the grass outside becomes wet from dew or rain, I have to pick my way around a parade of giant snails on the trail. Using the outdoor toilet can be an adventure, especially at night when I take my flashlight to shine into the bowl. So far I've found a slug, a frog, a snail, and one really gnarly cockroach lying in wait for me.

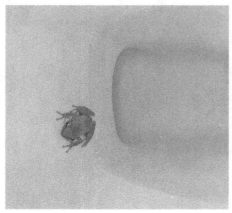

As the sun goes down, the jungle noise turns up. The infamous coqui frogs sing their resonant songs throughout the night while crickets add backup harmonies. And as the sun comes up, the neighborhood roosters add their voices to the chorus.

The one-room cabin has

screened windows on every wall, along with a screened door. Although there are blinds installed on most windows, I've just been leaving everything open all day and night to keep that sultry air flowing through. I lay in bed at night and enjoy the moonlight streaming in, and fall asleep to the jungle music all around me.

So I go about my usual business day to day around the cabin – preparing meals, doing laundry, taking photos, reading and writing – all in the buff. (I am so going to miss this place when I go back to the comparatively harsh climate of Seattle!) I do put on clothes when I venture out into civilization each day, but this hippie-centric district of Puna on the Big Island is super laid back. A sarong and flip flops is business casual in this part of the world.

I'm shifting from tourist mode into life mode. I'm no longer taking tours and visiting museums. Instead I'm spending time each day reviewing my writings and envisioning my book. I'm collecting ideas and inspirations from this process of planning and travel, and figuring out what I want to say when all is said and done...

Day 160 - Uncle Robert's (Kalapana, Hawaii)
Thursday, August 18, 2016

I don't personally have an Uncle Robert, but in Hawaii the concept of 'ohana (family) extends well beyond blood relations to embrace the wider community, guests included.

Uncle Robert was the patriarch of the tiny village of Kalapana, located at the end of the red road on the east side of the Big Island of Hawaii. A field of hardened lava ends the red road and serves as a parking lot for the hundreds (sometimes thousands, I'm told) of locals and guests who flock to this festive Uncle Robert's farmers' market on Wednesday nights and Sunday mornings.

Kalapana feels like a remote location, and yet this twice-weekly party is well known to locals as well as the local tourist industry. There's no roasted pig pulled up out of the ground and no native women dancing the hula while wearing grass skirts, but the tradition of the luau - community gathering to feast and celebrate with music and dance - was definitely in full force.

There's a bar that accepts "donations" for drinks – I'm guessing that's a licensing issue that prevents the actual sale of liquor. There are dozens of vendors who set up tables under awnings and tarps that provide semi-permanent shelter from the blazing sun and frequent rains.

You can find clothing, books, handmade soaps, incense, jewelry, local produce and flowers, glass pipes, and much more. There are also many food vendors offering a wide variety of ethnic special-ties, hamburgers, spam sushi, fruit smoothies, wood-fired pizzas, and fresh coconuts hacked open right in front of you.

And of course, there's a stage for music and an open floor for dancing. A section of long picnic tables provides seating for din-ers and locals who have brought their own picnics. In the spirit of reusing and recycling, a row of bucket seats removed from a va-riety of vehicles lines one side of the dining area to offer addition-al comfortable seating.

My parents and I showed up early and claimed seats at the picnic tables to enjoy the music, including a great Hawaiian blues num-ber about the very event we were attending. The crowd poured in at a steady pace and within an hour, it became hard to move between the tables.

We wanted to try the famous Hawaiian nachos – a heaping plate of fried wonton chips covered in BBQ pulled pork, tomatoes, and a creamy red sauce meant to look like lava pouring down from the mountain of chips - but the popular dish was already sold out. Next time!

Day 164 - Hot Lava
Sunday, August 21, 2016

Yesterday my parents and I had the privilege of witnessing the birth of new land on the Big Island of Hawaii. Mount Kīlauea continues her slow and steady eruption of molten lava, moving down the mountain and into the sea to form an ever-evolving coastline minute by minute.

Many other tourists took the hard way and hiked ten miles round trip under the relentless sunshine to perch hazardously on the unstable cliffs looking down on the lava flow. We took the safer and far easier option of going out to see the lava by boat.

I found a company that caters to no more than six passengers at a time – each with their own 360-degree swiveling arm chair on deck to take in all the action. Other companies offered sardine-packed boat tours for up to 50 passengers at a time for nearly the same price, so we were very happy with our good fortune!

The 40-minute boat ride out to the lava flow was a lot like riding a bucking bronco between two fire hoses. The ocean surrounding the island is active even on the nicest days and our 25-foot boat tackled each swell with gusto, rising and falling with the water as we rose and fell in our chairs.

We enjoyed the view and the sea spray along the way, leaning eagerly over the rail to catch glimpses of the steaming coastline as we approached the lava site. When we drew near, it became a full sensory experience.

The burning lava gave off enough heat that we could feel it from our safe distance of 20-30 feet away. We could smell the sulfur in the thick billowing clouds of steam rising from the juncture of lava and ocean, and hear the quiet sizzle beneath the loud crashing of ocean waves against the cliff. The red glow of lava dripped from the cliff tops and oozed out over the surface of the newly forming land to meet the sea.

Our boat stayed near the lava, bobbing in the surf for at least twenty minutes while we all took photos and videos. The seawater on the surface was the temperature of a nice toasty hot tub,

170

even from thirty feet away. Our Captain was diligent about keeping an eye on our position to assure that we stayed at a safe distance while allowing us to get close enough for a mind blowing firsthand experience.

As the waves crashed against the flow I could see tiny splashes of lava kicked up in the surf, cooling into black pebbles as they fell into the ocean. We also witnessed the spectacle of floating chunks of a'a lava suspended on the surface of the ocean, which is a rare occurence only possible where hot lava meets a body of water.

The boat ride can be a little rough on those of us unaccustomed to life on the sea, and so our guide passed around snacks and beverages to help settle our stomachs for the bumpy 40-minute return to land. I munched on my goldfish crackers and waved aloha to Pele, goddess of the volcano, as the boat pulled away and the lava flow disappeared into the distance behind us.

Day 168 - Off Grid
Thursday, August 25, 2016

I've been living "off grid" for just over two weeks now and it's definitely been a learning experience! My tiny cabin in the jungle is powered by two solar panels and provided with water through a rain catchment system. Being in Hawaii, both sun and rain are usually abundant and so this is a practical system.

However, living with these systems requires an awareness of natural resources and a major shift of habits because I'm accustomed to the mindless never-ending availability of water and power from the grid.

I've learned to avoid flushing the toilet too many times on dry days, since that leaves me with no water for washing my hands afterwards. Both the modern commode and beautiful art glass sink are provided with water direct from a rain catchment tank above the "outhouse." I have the option to manually refill the catchment tank from the large cistern that supplies the kitchen sink and outdoor shower, but I prefer trying to shift my usage to match nature's availability.

Over the last few days of dark gray skies and steady rain, I've also learned that solar power has its limits. The first thing to stop was the ceiling fan. Then the lights in the cabin wouldn't turn on. And last, the small energy-efficient fridge could only run for a few seconds before exhausting itself with a sigh.

My habit is now to light an oil lamp after the sun goes down. It creates a beautiful atmosphere, and provides enough light for whatever I'm doing in the evening. The owner of the cabin also suggested that I could unplug the fridge at night, which retains its cool temperature into the morning hours, further conserving power.

So I'm learning to live with greater attention to the natural world around me, and learning to balance my needs and habits with what nature has to offer at any given time. It's a definite shift from my usual blind consumption of grid resources, and a valuable lesson overall.

Day 174 – Lavascape
Wednesday, August 31, 2016

Yesterday my friend Amy and I hiked down into the caldera (bottom of Kilauea crater) to experience a completely alien landscape. A magical walk through the jungle under giant hanging ferns and lush tropical foliage led us to the vast open space of the crater.

The ground was hardened lava as far as the eye could see, into the steaming horizon in the far distance. A few varieties of hardy plants sparsely populated the caldera, creating surprising bursts of green and red to break up the solid black of the hardened lava. The caldera was bordered on our nearest side by the high rocky cliffs of the crater's edge.

We were both stunned into reverent silence. The wind was whipping across the landscape and we were the only people around. I was compelled to shout out in my loudest voice, "hello!", only to hear my own voice rebound back to me in fading echoes. We each spent some time calling out to play with the echo effect, making our small presence known in the immense openness of our surroundings.

As is my usual practice when visiting sites of stunning natural beauty and spiritual significance, I brought a gift for the spirits of the place. In this case, my gift was offered to Pele, goddess of the volcano.

The ground formed by the lava is riddled with many cracks, caves, and fissures. I found a wide opening to a shallow cave and sat in brief meditation to connect before leaving my offering of an iridescent sea shell collected from a beach in New Zealand.

The feeling of standing in that huge crater, unlike anything either of us had ever experienced before, made us want to stay as long as possible to soak it all in. But with the day growing short, and a hike back up through the thick jungle still to go before the sun set, we waved goodbye to the goddess and made our way back to the surface.

We enjoyed dinner while the sun was setting and then headed farther up the mountain to the lava viewing area just as darkness set in. Even from the parking lot, we could see the eerie orange glow through the steam venting up from the open crater. Tourists from all over the world were milling about, taking photos and gazing in rapt attention at the amazing phenomenon in the distance.

Although the actual churning and burning red/black lava couldn't be seen at this time because too much lava has been flowing down to the coast, the nighttime glow was enchanting. The steam billowed and rolled, moving like a living creature as it rose from the mouth of the crater. The lava beneath the visible rim cast an ethereal glow to the steam, reflecting upwards to color the fluffs of cloud hovering above the mountain.

Adding to the atmosphere, the deep black of the night sky above us shone with a plethora of stars. The Milky Way was visible, as were countless constellations, planets, and satellites. With the luminous lava in front of us, and the splendor of stars above us, all we could do was bask in the incredible beauty of this world.

Day 178 - Retreat Forward (Homeward Bound)
Sunday, September 04, 2016

I'm two days away from completing my journey. That blows my mind at least as much as leaving for this trip in the first place! So many new experiences have enriched my life over the last six months. I've made so many incredible new friends. My perspective has been broadened tremendously.

One of my goals is to complete a full circle around this planet. A circle begins and ends at the exact same point, and that point for me is my home. There are many places around the world that I love and would really enjoy staying in longer, but home is special and calls to my heart in ways that no other place on Earth can match.

As much fun and excitement as I've had, it's time for me to go home. I yearn for the comforts of my own space and for stability upon which I can rebuild my life. In order to continue growing, I have to go back. In order to move forward... I must retreat.

Now that my journey is nearly finished, I face the challenge of creating a new life for myself. I won't be going back to the same work, the same lifestyle, which I left behind half a year ago. My next goal is to support myself financially with my writing.

Before I departed on this journey, I came up with a somewhat lofty list of conditions to meet as I start making money again. I'll share that list with you here, in part to announce my intentions to the world... and in part to keep myself honest when the temptation to go back to "the usual" gets too strong.

Conditions for Earning Income in My Ideal Lifestyle:

1. Work from any Wi-Fi enabled location
2. Work autonomously during whatever hours I choose
3. Complete creative projects on reasonable deadlines
4. Enjoy sufficient compensation to live and travel comfortably
5. Develop relationships of collaboration, support, and trust with my professional peers
6. Develop professional reputation for excellence and integrity
7. Interact with others whose goals and values are in harmony with my own
8. Easily balance a relaxed and healthy lifestyle while advancing my professional achievements

That's it! Eight simple little requirements (*insert sarcasm here*) for an ideal life of authenticity, health, and happiness.

I'll keep blogging as I reintegrate back into "the real world" and continue pursuing my goals.

To be continued…

THE FINAL STATISTICS:

$27,941.............Total Spend (average $155 per day)
435 Hours ....Spent in Transit
36,100 Miles....Traveled Point to Point

$10,883 ....Accommodations (180 nights)
$6,726 ....Travel (Point-to-Point =$6,118 / Local = $608)
$2,506 ....Experience (Tours, Museums, Adventures, etc.)
$2,110 ....Food/Beverage (Restaurants, Grocery)
$2,886 ....Cash (Food, Experience, Stuff, Misc.)
$1,828 ....Stuff (Gifts, Souvenirs)
$968 ....Miscellaneous (Visas, Insurance, etc.)
$34 ....Foreign ATM fees

276 ....Hours over Sea
85 ....Hours over Land
74 ....Hours in the Air
4 ....Equator Crossings
1 ....International Date Line Crossing
13 ....Countries Visited (including home country)

1 ....Overall Super Awesome Life Experience

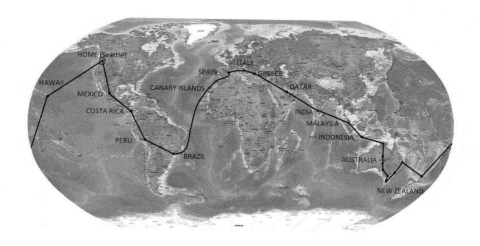

To see full color photos and videos of the journey:
https://www.youtube.com/watch?v=AXrG5FV4Y1M

PART THREE:

AND THEN...?

Home Day Three: Re-Entry (Seattle, USA)
Saturday, September 10, 2016

I'm working on photos and writing from my journey. I'm day-dreaming and researching ALL sorts of potential paths I could take while constantly reminding myself that I have plenty of time.

There's no need to rush, and not everything has to be established right this very minute. Building a new income source and life-style around it is no small project! I've contacted an accountant for a consultation on getting started (taxes, etc.) in the business of freelance writing.

And I'm settling back into my home - rearranging, cleaning, and spreading my energy around as I'm unpacking and making room for new items from my travels. I'm going out for groceries and other home/personal maintenance tasks. I'm driving my car, checking my mail, and sleeping in my own bed (oh, the bliss!) every night.

I guess all that means... back to "normal?"

My mood is still very high. I'm delighted to be home and even more delighted to have the time available to sort through my many experiences of the last six months.

There is some very minor anxiety around what to do for income in the near future, but I have more than one backup plan if I need income in a hurry, and I came back under budget so I have more padding than expected. I saved enough money to buy myself some time to do things right.

I'm just taking it day by day, letting myself relax and play as much as I work, even though there's still more to be done.

Home Day Fifteen: Time and Productivity
Wednesday, September 21, 2016

I've been back home for two whole weeks now. It feels good and I'm slowly settling back into my space, but the thing I notice the most is how oddly time seems to be moving since my return. Days fly by with hardly any notice, but the hours of those days pass slowly.

It feels like I just got back, but two weeks is the entire amount of time that I spent in each of the two communities I visited on my journey, and it felt like a lot can happen in that timeframe. I have this big to-do list in my mind, but I'm noticing so much time can slip by without getting to those items because I'm not feeling any urgency.

In my past professional life, I was known as "blindingly efficient." I never missed a deadline and had a reputation for reliability. I showed up early and took only short breaks to assure that I could accomplish my heavy workload. My attention was focused and dedicated.

Now I sleep late every day. I linger over my morning cup of tea with nothing more demanding than facebook to claim my attention. I eventually get around to doing chores or delving into projects or research, only to emerge several hours later after my body starts complaining for a break. Time drifts, rather than being driven.

My social calendar is filling up as I continue reaching out to reconnect with friends, but other than that, there is absolutely no external schedule driving my days right now. There is no weekend – no Monday, no Friday, no difference between days... other than traffic on the freeways. The only structure my life currently follows is the rising and setting of the sun, and my body's clock telling me when to eat and sleep.

So I'm experiencing quite a contrast to the far more rigid lifestyle I lived when last I was home. The freedom is dizzying and, admittedly, I'm still doing a fair amount of sitting around binging on Netflix and playing video games right now.

I know the time is coming when I'll need to focus my attention on being productive again – and that it will feel really good to make that shift when I do. But for now... I'm just drifting a bit while opening myself for the universe to present opportunities.

I met with my new accountant yesterday to better understand how my finances/taxes will operate once I begin earning income outside of standard employment situations. Next on the agenda is to get myself set up as a tax-identified business with both federal and state agencies, then on to setting up banking, and re-designing my website to include donation features.

So... yea. I'm doing a whole lotta nothing, but I'm also getting stuff done. Life is good!

Home Month One: Finding My Way
Friday, October 07, 2016

As of today I've been back home exactly one month. We have plenty of natural beauty here in the great Pacific Northwest, and I continue "embracing the world" even in my own backyard. Please enjoy this photo, taken during a recent sunset over Lake Washington.

I've taken a lot of time to think about what direction I want my life to go from this point, and have been listening to my feelings to help guide my choices (in addition to ridiculous amounts of research, of course). So I've decided that I'm a writer and that I'm going to build a livelihood out of that.

I don't expect that I'm going to immediately write a best-selling book and live off royalties for years (although that does sound nice), and I recognize that a writer generally has to start at the bottom just like any other profession.

It seems logical to start looking for dues to pay, so to speak. I'm now looking for those entry-level opportunities for freelance writers - and there are plenty to be found. But while real opportunities are definitely out there, so are the get-rich-quick schemes.

The other day I watched an infomercial claiming that I could make up to $30,000 each for writing letters for direct marketers! (Oh, how I wish I could believe that.) The cheery voice in the ad assured me that many people were making six or even seven figures per year just writing letters. One guy only works an hour each week!

The nearly hour-long video was spinning a beautiful image of every lazy person's dream... "and you don't even have to be a good writer!"

Hold on, stop the boat. You don't have to be a good writer? But I am a good writer! No, no, no. Even if I did believe their fairytale about earning oodles of money for very little work, I'm going to need some appreciation for my creative efforts. If they don't need good writers, then I will seek elsewhere.

I continue submitting resumes and samples for interesting opportunities, remembering my list of goals all the while. I found a promising situation with a company that contracts out small research projects, and took two hours to complete a test assignment for them. They welcomed me to their collective of researchers, and set me loose to choose my first paying assignment.

The assignments are said to take between one to three hours to complete, depending on complexity. Each project is also paid according to its degree of complexity, so simple questions should be lower paying. I chose one of the three low-pay questions and got to work.

I was making good progress up until I couldn't find a source for one of the requested data points. Then it took a while to get myself setup on the support network chatroom to request help from other researchers, but I finally got the answers I needed.

About three hours from the time I started, I submitted my finished research project for a grand total of $17 compensation. ($5.50/hour)

And then... I received a rejection notice, because the work I submitted didn't meet unstated requirements. Before I was able to make the suggested changes and additions, another writer had claimed the assignment. My pay for those three hours of wasted effort was $0.

This morning I sent my own rejection notice back to the company, complete with data points to illustrate each reason I wouldn't continue working for them. Back to the search for income!

Home Week Six: Freedom
Tuesday, October 18, 2016

I had a lot of fun in my travels and was pretty happy most of the time, but since I've been back home... my level of Happy has definitely climbed skyward. My mood is hovering around 30,000 feet over the ground. I'm reveling in this sensation of lightness, feeling like there is nothing holding me down.

Because it's in my nature, I've been pondering what's at the root of this extraordinary happiness I'm feeling. Where is this coming from? What is so different about my life right here and now...?

There's the fact that literally nothing is weighing on me right now. No deadlines, no expectations (other than my own), and no responsibilities beyond caring for myself and my home. No pressing needs fill my thoughts. No worries cloud my mind. I am unburdened.

Part of that is the natural result of vacation afterglow and my current lack of job responsibility, but part of it is the result of a conscious positive outlook.

I choose to believe that everything I need is going to work out fine, even though I have absolutely no idea at this exact moment how that's going to happen. I could choose to let that unknown cause me stress, but that stress would serve no good purpose.

And so the question of my future only lingers in my mind as a curiosity, rather than stalking me like a hungry predator. I'm just so delighted to be back in my own home, closer to loved ones, and with the incredible opportunity to reform my life into exactly what I want it to be.

Now, I know my current emotional condition can't (and shouldn't) last forever. I'll eventually return to working and volunteering and all of those things that make up a worthwhile and fulfilling life, even though each commitment and responsibility carries some burden of weight.

My life will be full and heavy again, probably before I even realize what's happening. And that's a good thing! But for now... for this brief span of time while I'm still living outside of a long term routine... the freedom is exquisite.

Home Week Ten: COPE-ing
Saturday, November 12, 2016

As an American traveling through foreign lands in the months leading up to our recent presidential election, I heard the same question from so many people in different countries. "So... Trump. What are you Americans thinking??"

I cringed every time I was associated with Mr. Trump as an American. The qualities of empathy, integrity, and kindness that are so important to me appear to be completely lacking from his character. I don't respect his choices as an individual and I certainly don't want him making leadership choices on behalf of me and my country. And yet... he is now our next legally elected leader.

Like so many others, I'm having a hard time with this new reality. Roughly half of my fellow Americans cast their vote in favor of a man who is an excellent example of the worst of humanity. They

185

chose to bestow power and prestige upon him - to make a role model out of him. That is hard to accept.

Feelings of anger and betrayal towards friends and family of conflicting opinions are impossible to escape, and everyone is struggling to deal with the overwhelming emotions surrounding this election.

The stereotype of the ignorant, self-centered American is alive and well. I've been traveling internationally for the last twelve years and have frequently encountered people who tell me they're pleasantly surprised to find that an American could be anything other than rude and obnoxious. Our citizens have an international reputation, and I'm sorry to say that we've earned it.

So what can I do as a citizen of a nation with so many other citizens who hold values counter to my own? The spoiled brat in me wants to take my ball and go home. "You guys are mean and I don't want to play with you anymore. You can find me in Canada when you want to apologize."

Thankfully, I'm not a petulant child and life is too complicated to simply walk away from it anyway. But the emotions remain, and the need is strong to somehow distance myself from what I perceive as a growing culture of ignorance and hatred.

So here's my strategy: from now on, I am a Citizen of Planet Earth (COPE). I'm still an American as much as I'm a woman, a sister, a friend, and more... but I'm building a new mindset.

My home is this entire planet, and that is where my loyalties live. I can only systemically vote by ballot in the one small geography of my residence, but I can vote with my words and actions every day – demonstrating the values of a Citizen of Planet Earth:

1. The Earth is our only home and the preservation of its health and well-being is our Utmost Top Priority.
2. Every part of the Earth (human, animal, plant, land, sea, sky) deserves respect.
3. Cooperation (working together) is valued over competition (working against).

4. Words have great power, which must be used responsibly.

So that's how I'm COPE-ing. I'm solidifying my own core values and I'm sticking to them. Now more than ever, it's important to know our selves, and to be true to ourselves. This world is going to be topsy turvy for a while and it's going to need some pillars to hold us steady.

By holding strong to our own values, we can be the pillars. I'm a citizen of this beautiful planet, just like you. My priority is the well-being of the world and every being in it.

Home Week Fifteen: Solstice
Wednesday, December 21, 2016

Today is the Winter Solstice in the northern hemisphere where I live. This is the shortest day of the year and the longest night. From now until the Summer Solstice six months away, things will only get lighter and brighter. This is the second Winter Solstice that I've celebrated in 2016. The first was in Australia's winter in June.

I've been home for just over three months now, and still feeling like I'm regaining my balance in this part of world after traveling around the rest of the planet.

Every other year for the past couple of decades, I have "walked the wheel of the year" in my home location – I've practiced conscious awareness of the cycle of seasons as they repeat predictably with every complete revolution of the Earth.

And yet before I traveled, it never actually occurred to me that many other parts of the world don't share this same seasonal experience. I celebrated the Spring Equinox near the Equator, where there are no seasons at all. Every day is the Equinox in Costa Rica! India and Southeast Asia have wet and dry seasons, hot and warm seasons; which doesn't compare to the four-part cycle of more extreme latitudes.

Celebrating the solstices (shortest and longest days), equinoxes (equal hours of day and night), and "cross-quarter" days between those points has set the rhythm of my years for a long time. I feel like I got off the beat during my journey, and that I temporarily experienced so many different natural rhythms of the climates around me that I can hardly remember my own anymore.

It's been said that, "you can't go home again." I think you can return home, but that your perception may be so altered that home doesn't feel the same. Old routines feel both familiar and alien. There really is no going back, but my journey is all about moving forward anyway.

The battle between going back to comfortable security (aka: a standard job) and pursuing my dream to live the lifestyle of a freelance writer continues to rage daily in my mind. The lure of a steady paycheck, benefits like health insurance and paid holidays, the ability to plan for my future... are all very strong motivators. But as easy as it would be to make the choice to take a regular job, that would feel like failure.

And so I persevere, stumbling around online and learning everything I can about people who are currently doing what I want to be doing. I put aside my aversion to business social networking and built myself a robust profile on LinkedIn. I'm pursuing opportunities that can only result in very low-paying work, but that will also build my professional portfolio and add to my credibility as a writer.

Project Retreat Forward continues and so does my blog. The posts are less frequent now that I'm not adventuring in exotic destinations every day, but the story continues. This is a journey not just of miles traveled and wonders visited, but of rebuilding my life around my dreams.

Stay tuned as I keep trying to figure out this whole Life thing...

Home Week Seventeen: New Year
Saturday, December 31, 2016

At this time last year I was barely two and a half months away from leaving a stressful job and embarking on my grand adventure. I was buzzing with excitement and anticipation. I knew that my coming year would be amazing and life changing, come what may.

And here I am now: my plan executed and my travel complete. After nearly four months at home, I'm past the re-entry phase and now into dreaming, researching, and planning for the future that I want to build. That may all sound great on paper, but it feels like floundering without a firm direction. I feel like I didn't plan far enough ahead.

The life of a writer is much like the life of an artist or actor – we pour our hearts and souls onto a canvas for the world to see... and to judge. And perhaps reject. Repeatedly.

Creating art simply for the sake of creating doesn't run into that problem so much, but when trying to get paid for one's art, when asking the world to agree that what we create has value, when trying to earn enough to make a living from art... rejection becomes a regular occurrence. Self-doubt begins to creep in. Releasing the angst felt after each rejection becomes a major act of personal will.

I suppose that this is one of the prices that must be paid for freedom, as opposed to the relative comfort and security of a day job with a steady paycheck. Building a career from nothing is very different than stepping into an open role in an established organization. I have the wild freedom of doing whatever, whenever, wherever I want... but the discipline to be productive is also entirely my responsibility.

To be a writer, one must write. (Seems pretty straightforward, right?) Looking for paid work as a writer isn't writing, although its a necessary task. Networking with other writers and learning the business side of things isn't writing either, but is vital to my success. I'm learning the elements that all come together to support the job of Writer, and I'm structuring my new workday to meet these responsibilities.

So with the new year, I'll start my new day job. As with Project Retreat Forward, I've hired myself and the pay is lousy, but the work supports my goals. Each day I'll devote two and a half hours to actively writing, plus 45 minutes of searching for paid work, plus 45 minutes of networking or business learning activity. (All estimates subject to change, but I gotta start somewhere!)

Sure that's only four hours per day, but that is solid concentrated work time, without the many distractions and interruptions that come with an office job. Instead of commuting, I can spend that time taking a long afternoon walk. Instead of hours of meetings, I can spend that time catching up with friends and family. Instead of being flooded with the minutiae of company politics, my mind is free to linger on more inspiring subjects.

I don't have an income yet, but I'm living my dream anyway. I can't live this way forever, but I guess I'm still riding that wave of faith from my giant leap forward. I believe that this is the path that leads where I want to go. Here's hoping that by this time next year, I'll be fully supporting myself with my writing!

"Fake it until you make it."

"You never know until you try."

"Build it and they will come."

(OK, maybe that last quote isn't as applicable, but it came from a great movie!)

Home Week Nineteen: On the Hunt
Sunday, January 15, 2017

In my last blog, I wrote of being uncomfortable drifting along without a solid plan. Then I went on to outline a very reasonable plan to live my days as a writer, exercising my self-discipline to create a productive routine. I followed that plan for precisely one day.

It's not that I lack self-discipline, but that I need more purpose than "just do it" to sustain my motivation. Daily writing is a fantastic practice, but in no way guarantees that an income will result from my considerable efforts. And since my primary goal right now is to build a sustainable lifestyle, which requires considerable income... it's back to the drawing board for a new plan.

At the same time, I'm reminded how much more difficult the simple things in life are when you're poor. I'm very happy living a low-spend lifestyle when I have a financial cushion, but then there's the frightening prospect of that same lifestyle with no savings and very little income to fall back on.

My current no-income status allows me to take advantage of free health insurance through my state to avoid the federal penalty for not being insured. Except that I worked part time for two months and failed to report that income, and so was kicked off the insurance plan. It took four phone calls, several days, and a letter stating that I'm self-employed with no current income to re-instate the insurance plan.

But even when I start making money, then the self-employment tax kicks in. A regular employee may pay 15% federal tax on their wages. People who are self-employed pay that 15%, and then an additional 15% on top of it. And once I start making money, then I'm required to report my earnings every month and have the cost of my mandatory insurance increased accordingly. The system makes it very difficult to succeed as self-employed.

My thoughts drift back to the day job option. With great reluctance, I pulled up LinkedIn and perused the twelve listings that popped up on my account. A job for a Proposal Writer caught my eye. I did that job for four years with my former employer, and it qualifies as writing!

I started researching the company, and was greatly impressed by their stated values and exceptionally generous benefits, as well as by the great satisfaction ratings reported by a high percentage of employees.

Checking that job opportunity against my ideal criteria, I was excited to see that it could meet every objective! Of course, this must be fate dropping perfection in my lap. (Wohoo!)

So I waited with baited breath for that call asking me to interview for the job that will solve all my worries. And I waited. Then I figured out that I could login to their online application system and found… "Not Accepted" as my application status. (*crushing disappointment*)

I guess that would have been too easy anyway, right?

So now I'm in the mindset again that a day job (aka: a level of income that can actually support my modestly comfortable life-style) is the best option right now to reach my goals. I aspire to sell my condo and buy a home with enough land for privacy and a garden. That goal isn't feasible without a stable income over a significant period of time.

If I choose the path of a freelance writer right now, I commit to more years of low income than my current savings can honestly support. If I choose the path of a job with enough income to allow for increased savings over time, then I can achieve my goal for a more pastoral home and hopefully gain more knowledge, experience, and network contacts to support writing income in my future.

My mind may change again tomorrow, but for now I'm on a job hunt. Dusting off the resume, reaching out to the world, and welcoming opportunity to come knocking.

I still have the time to wait for the right position, and I still have my criteria to guide me and assure that I'm moving in the right direction.

I'm doing my best to enjoy this time that I have to relax and prepare to take on my next challenge, without wallowing in the anxiety of needing to know what that's going to be and when it's going to happen...

Home Week Twenty-Three: Awareness
Saturday, February 11, 2017

I need to write about something that's been on my mind a lot lately. I sense a growing divide between two distinct mindsets in Western society. I'm sure that revelation comes as no surprise, because that divide is glaring and obvious to anyone who cares to look.

Deeper than any specific political issue, the divide appears to illuminate different core values. And yet when members of different factions do manage to bridge that divide with open honest conversations, they discover that their core values are actually very similar – safety and prosperity for ourselves and our communities, and the freedom to live however we choose.

The point where these values-oriented mindsets diverge is Awareness of consequences resulting from any course of action. To be clear, Awareness is not a yes/no condition. It's not a matter of either being aware or not being aware.

Awareness reflects varying levels of knowledge and understanding, and the ability to envision the ripple effect of consequences on the vast network of interconnections in society and our world.

To offer a political example, the choice to eliminate environmental protections in favor of making business easier and more profitable is lacking Awareness of consequences. Not only does that choice make business easier in the short term, but it also creates a long term (and potentially irreversible) negative impact on the environment that humanity relies on for sustenance. Such a choice would not be made by anyone who is truly aware of the greater consequences.

Empathy is the awareness of experience outside of ourselves, feeling or imagining the emotions of others, and being able to relate to pain that is not our own. Feeling empathy usually inspires compassion, because relating to someone else's pain motivates us to alleviate that pain. The personal experience of empathy/awareness is often painful.

I think this great divide that's growing greater every day is between those of very high awareness and those of very low awareness. Myself? I'm somewhere in the middle.

The injustice of social inequality for women and minorities of all kinds chafes at me. The inexcusable actions of our government (past and present) against our Native people hurts my heart. The laws being twisted to support the collection of power and wealth among very few individuals pisses me off.

But I can't allow myself to feel that all the time or I'd live my life in a constant state of righteous rage, which isn't who I want to be.

There are a growing number of highly aware people who are living in that righteous rage, feeding it and expressing it daily. I can't say that they're wrong in that choice, only that I don't have that kind of emotional stamina.

There are also a growing number of people who can't bear to accept more awareness of the pain and injustice apparent all around us. They choose to embrace the comfortable narrative that everything is OK, ignoring or explaining away any evidence to the contrary.

I can't really blame people for wanting to avoid pain and discomfort. I don't enjoy those conditions either, and like I said... I'm only partially aware myself, by choice.

Change takes time and involves a lot of work. It takes tremendous courage and strength to fully accept the reality of our society's darkest flaws and failures, and then to step up and make the effort to grow into healthier ways of living together.

We're all at different stages of personal development, and each of us gets to choose how much energy we devote to each important aspect of our lives. Some of us are compelled to fully embrace awareness – and all of the pain and struggle that goes with it. Some of us are compelled to ignore awareness – because accepting it is too much to even contemplate. And most of us are somewhere in between – aware enough to feel the pain, and uncomfortable enough to want it gone.

Objectively, I can't say that embracing awareness or remaining comfortable is a right or wrong choice. Everyone must do what they personally feel is right. But for myself, I can say that I'd much rather live in a society where we practice conscious awareness of how our choices impact each other and the world around us.

One Year After Departure
Sunday, March 12, 2017

On this day last year, I was finally setting off on my grand adventure. Six months of travel, twelve foreign countries, four equator crossings, and one trip back in time over the international dateline later, I arrived back home. Another six months later, and here I am still trying to find my new direction.

I'd love to be able to neatly conclude this story by telling you that my journey brought everything into crystal clear focus for me, and that I came home knowing exactly what I want to do now and exactly how I'm going to achieve those goals. That would be awesome, but this isn't that kind of fairy tale.

One of my most cherished personal values, which is reflected in the mission statement of Project Retreat Forward, is personal growth and development. I'm not talking about taking classes and workshops, earning certificates and degrees. I'm talking about taking all of life as a learning opportunity – actively seeking the lessons that present themselves in the mundane and in the extraordinary. I'm talking about being both an observer and active participant in the human experience.

As far as that value goes, I feel like a smashing success. More than ever, I'm moving through life with my senses open and my mind clear, taking it all in. I feel at peace within myself, even with the storm of emotions raging around me in these turbulent times. My faith in my own choices remains solid.

Many spiritual traditions encourage some variation of quieting our minds so that we may hear the "still, small voice" within ourselves. Perhaps the greatest lesson that I've taken from these years of planning and executing this dream-fueled journey is better listening to that voice as my source of guidance.

I'll share this secret with you that took me so long to learn... that voice doesn't speak in words. It speaks in sensations – feelings. I've learned to listen closely to my body to help guide my choices.

Imagine your body as a metal detector, randomly exploring the terrain around you until you get the "ping" that tells you you're on the right track. Once you've got that initial ping, then just keep exploring and making course adjustments until the pings get stronger. A ping could be a feeling in your gut, a tingling on your skin, a light that catches your eye... pretty much any sensation, up to your own interpretation.

It sounds overly simple, and honestly, it is. That's one of those things about profound truths - they tend to be embarrassingly obvious once you find them.

Learning to listen to my body, learning to understand how that still small voice speaks within me, is an ongoing process. But without fail, my body feels good after I make good choices, and my body feels bad when I make bad choices. From that starting point, it's possible to begin understanding greater complexities in my body's communications.

I'm still exploring the terrain of my life, waiting for that ping to show me the right direction. I'm actively looking for full time work similar to what I used to do, even though I don't feel a ping, because it's the responsible thing to do and earning money is a great way to achieve certain goals. I'm also still dreaming - researching how to make my more ambitious hopes into realities, but no pings in that direction yet either.

So the search goes on, scanning for opportunities, listening closely for the slightest indication that I'm on the right track...

PING!
Friday, March 17, 2017

In my last blog I wrote of listening for that internal "ping" to let me know when I find a good choice. Well... PING! Not long after I wrote that, inspiration struck and I started researching a new idea.

196

Lately I've been thinking about one of my as-yet unfulfilled dreams – to own and operate a luxury camping retreat, much like the treehouses, tents, and cabins that I visited on my world journey. But given that my personal finances are limited, I don't have the option to simply build/buy my dream business and settle down into a life of bliss tomorrow. (Wouldn't that be nice?)

So how do I get from here to there? First of all, it seems like a good idea to gain some experience working in the industry, if I plan to invest my life savings and devote my blood, sweat and tears into manifesting this vision.

Working in the camping hospitality industry often means living at a campground property. Since most campgrounds feature some sort of natural beauty away from major civilization, living in that atmosphere is nothing but bonus for me!

To live and work amongst the campers, learning their ways so that I can better understand how to make them happy customers of my own business later, I need entrance to that community. And that means buying an RV!

So that's my plan. I'm now preparing to sell most of my possessions, rent out my condo to pay the mortgage, devote my remaining savings to transforming myself into a turtle (carrying my home on my back), and hit the road to find a campground that wants to give me a job.

After maybe three to five years, I'll have more of the knowledge and experience I need (not to mention industry networking), and I'll be able to trade my condo for a down payment on the beautiful piece of nature that will be my future home and business.

Project Retreat Forward will continue as the Road Trip Edition, following my transition from corporate condo-dweller to purveyor of relaxation and natural beauty. Once I really get going in the niche of writing about campgrounds and RV lifestyle, I hope to find sponsors to help support my blog and travels.

This decision is fresh. I'm still processing the "wow, am I really going to do this?" thoughts, which are now so familiar after my round-the-world adventure. But, yea. I'm really gonna do this. And my timeline is to be on the road by May 1st - only 6 weeks from now.

To be honest, I've been wanting to leave my condo for a long time. I've been pondering a big road trip for a long time. I've been trying to find a different lifestyle for a long time. Now is just the moment when the solution comes into focus and I pull the trigger after all that wind up.

I continue to Retreat Forward. I'm consciously moving my life in the direction that I want to go. Once again, that means leaving familiar comforts and securities behind.

Now I gather my courage, take a deep breath, and... GO!

PART FOUR:

AMERICAN ROAD TRIP (A.R.T.)

Retreat Forward: A.R.T. (American Road Trip)
Wednesday, April 05, 2017

It's been almost three weeks since I made the decision to sell most of my stuff and move into an RV full time. I've set an aggressive schedule to be on the road in another three weeks and there is SO much to do!!

By now, I've purchased my RV and I'm in the hiring process for workamping with a campground in the mountains surrounded by forest (yay!) I've gotten rid of books, DVDs, clothes, and other stuff I don't need, and there's still more to go - including all of my furniture.

I've driven the RV only once so far, and it was definitely nerve wracking. I'm sure it will get easier with practice, but for the moment... all I can do is white-knuckle through it.

As with any used vehicle, it needs some work before a big road trip. Leaving it to get brakes and tires replaced, transmission and oil serviced; cut into the time that I hoped to be renovating my new home.

Despite the anxiety of making all of these huge life changes in a very short span of time, I feel like the universe is conspiring in favor of my success. Even though this is all a bit crazy, it feels right.

When I let go of the analytical mind, let go of worrying about exactly how everything is going to work out, then I have a very strong sense that everything will work out perfectly in ways I don't know yet.

And honestly, I already made my way full circle around the planet on my own. Just driving around my own country should be a piece of cake (once I get past the fear of smashing my big bus into something.)

Project Retreat Forward was about throwing myself out there in the big wide world and growing from the wealth of experiences in different countries and cultures. Retreat Forward: A.R.T. (American Road Trip) is very similar, just driving around on one continent instead flying around the globe.

But more than that, the name I've chosen for this next part of my journey hints at the concept of living my life as art – as a continual creative expression of who I am and what I want to share with the world. Art is a thing of beauty and meaning, emotionally evocative and meant to inspire. Art can also be disturbing, stretching boundaries in uncomfortable ways, and meant to deliver a unique perspective.

This land is my canvas, and my footsteps (OK, maybe my tires) are the brush with which I'll paint. The encounters I have with people along the way will provide the glorious chaos of color, expanding my creation beyond even my own imagination.

All that and more... once I learn to drive this beast.

Launching the Maiden Voyage (Leavenworth)
Sunday, April 30, 2017

I feel like I've just completed a marathon. My body is bruised and abused, but my plan was executed according to schedule even if some details got deprioritized in the process.

Task #1 – Buy an RV and make it road worthy.

With a tremendous amount of support and guidance from my mom and dad (RVers with 25+ years of experience), the first task was accomplished. New parts installed, maintenance applied, and countless little exterior improvements made by my dad - and the rig was ready to go.

Task #2 – Renovate the RV interior to my satisfaction.

OK, so this didn't go as hoped. I did rip out the old carpet (with thanks to my sister and nephew for their assistance), and I installed new vinyl flooring that looked great... but then there were technical difficulties.

The slide-out room on my RV refused to slide-in once the flooring was installed. I devoted a whole day out of my very tight schedule to trying to find a good solution, and ended up removing several planks of flooring to make the slide work.

So the floor is only partially complete. There are still odd-shaped bare patches of floor around the edges, and none of the trim is installed yet. Too bad, because there are other items on the schedule. Moving on.

Task #3 – Drive the rig to a park near my condo for move-in/move-out.

My second time driving the rig wasn't bad. After about three hours of morning commuter traffic, I got it backed into my assigned site with the help of my dad and a neighbor who came out to help. (This is apparently a very common occurrence in RV parks. People want to help!)

Moving into the RV wasn't hard, just a lot of trips with loads of stuff that I needed to find places to stow away. Moving out of the condo was more challenging, given all of the furniture and loads of stuff to sell and give away. Furniture was still going out the door on the night before departure, and one big piece is still in there, but time marches on and departure won't be delayed for an armoire!

Task #4 – Get ready to roll.

The night before departure is when things really got stressful. I tested my slide-out in advance, just to make sure that I wouldn't have any problems in the morning.

There were problems. It wouldn't slide-in. It wouldn't even make a noise. There was just no response to the switch.

Recognizing that I was in over my head, I knocked on the door of one of my neighbors I met last week – a retired electrical engineer and RVer with 30 years of experience. He helped me poke around outside under the slide-out to better understand the mechanism, and used some tools to test the current going to and from the switch that wasn't getting a response. He showed me that there was an electrical problem and I resigned myself to the necessity of crawling under the rig to manually retract the slide with his help in the morning.

The morning of departure I got everything in the rig stowed away and ready to travel. I went down my "pre-flight checklist" to assure that all systems were ready to hit the road.

And then I sat waiting... and waiting... for my neighbor to emerge and assist me with the two-person job of manually moving the slide.

I finally got tired of waiting and decided to try the switch in a futile hope that something might work. Low and behold, the slide made a noise. (It's alive!) And yet it still wouldn't close, so I ruthlessly yanked out the remaining floor planks near the slide edge and pushed the button once more with baited breath.

It worked! IT WORKED!!!

With that feat accomplished, I was ready to pull the rig out of my site and hook up my towed car ("toad"). But of course, I've never actually done that before. Fortunately, another neighbor popped up who happens to have lots of experience with the exact tow bar I have on my car, and together we got it hooked up and tested.

Task #5 – Destination Leavenworth

I got on the road and was feeling good. No problems merging with the freeway, no problems changing lanes. Made it to the country highway that goes almost to my destination.

My speed was always 10mph or more under the posted limit, but the other drivers dealt with it. Going up the mountain, it was a struggle to keep up to 35mph in a 60mph zone, but we just kept chugging away.

Dragging all that weight up a mountain took a lot of fuel and I was looking at my dwindling gas gauge with concern. I was delighted to find a gas station just before the last turn towards the campground.

On my first approach, I was too far from the pump. I couldn't back up with the toad attached and I was looking around the small parking lot trying to make a plan for a closer approach. It looked like I had enough room to make a full circle, so I went for it. That's when I realized that I couldn't complete my circle because of one car in the way.

Feeling utterly embarrassed by my newbie ineptitude, I went into the restaurant and asked for help. They found the owner of the car, who quickly moved out of my way. I was able to complete my tight circle and successfully filled my tank. Whew!

204

Back on the road, I was following the directions to the campground that google gave me. I made my final turn, but didn't see anything looking like check-in. I continued going straight down the paved road, which then became a gravel road. I had a sinking feeling that I was going the wrong way, but there was nothing to do except keep going forward and hope to find a place that I could turn around.

Seeing a dirt road next to a wide flat field, I decided to try it on the chance that I could turn in the field. Then the dirt road became narrower and fenced on either side. I was trapped, with nowhere to go.

It was then that I noticed a man in a pickup truck behind me. The gentleman helped me unhitch my car from the rig, and I backed it down the dirt road to the intersection with the wider gravel road. Then he directed me as I backed the rig down that same narrow dirt track, around a corner, and back onto the gravel road where we re-attached the toad and I continued on my way with a wave of thanks. I was not the first wayward traveler he'd rescued!

After all that, it was smooth sailing for the 2-3 minutes it took to reach the real park entrance. I chose my site, backed in the rig with the assistance of a new coworker, got all my systems hooked up, then crashed for the night after a quick trip to a nearby small town for provisions.

The music of rain falling on my roof and frogs singing outside my bedroom window lulled me to sleep. I woke up to birds singing, the wind whispering through the tall trees, and snow-capped mountain peaks glowing in the morning sun. That's what I'm talking about!

I feel like I moved mountains to get here, but the effort is worth it.

New Lifestyle
Thursday, May 11, 2017

Two weeks into my new lifestyle and things are going great. My commute is now a ten-minute walk through sun dappled forest and open meadow under a glorious blue sky with majestic mountain peaks in the background. The guests and coworkers who share my days are generally interesting, friendly, and fun people to be around. It's a laid back and peaceful atmosphere, just the way I like it.

This campground is divided into three main areas and I chose my site in the most remote of the three, in a "neighborhood" populated mostly by fellow park employees and full-time guests. There's a sense of community here, with lots of familiar faces greeting each other every day. My neighborhood is also the closest to the network of hiking trails on the 300 acres of park, which is an added bonus for me.

I'm figuring out where to find groceries in this sparsely serviced region, and how to feed myself three meals a day without eating out and frequenting the deli counter.

I used to be on the go all the time and it was easy to eat one or two meals of take-out or prepared meals every day. But now I have to make a special trip out of the park and at least 10-30 minutes away to get groceries or take-out, and my budget is more limited. The time has come to learn how to eat-in.

Fortunately, I now have a partner in some of my cooking endeavors. My friend and fellow full-time RVer, Dave, arrived to work here for the summer just a few days after I did. His RV is parked in the site next to mine, which makes dinner collaborations quick and easy.

But this lifestyle does have its drawbacks. In the ten years that I lived in my condo, nothing ever broke or failed. The heating always came on when I turned the dial. The hot water was readily available and consistent in temperature. The toilet flushed every time without complaint. None of these things are true of life in my RV.

Knowing what to do when problems bubble up (now I'm having flashbacks of yesterday's toilet incident), is vitally important to this lifestyle. There are so many skills that I need to build in a hurry!

When the toilet problem arose I really tried not to play the damsel in distress card, but my neighbor played the gallant knight anyway, stepping in to assist with the issue that was beyond my former capabilities to fix (and honestly... just too icky to contemplate.)

But now I know what to do next time, and I'll just keep learning with each incident until the RV and I come to some understanding about how things are supposed to work around here.

Plot Twist
Sunday, May 28, 2017

All good stories have unexpected twists and turns and it seems that mine is no exception. Project Retreat Forward began as the "unfolding story of one woman's personal journey to embrace the world", but as I've embarked on this next stage in the Retreat Forward process the perfect companion to my journey has appeared. And so this is no longer the tale of just one person.

In my last blog, I mentioned that a friend had arrived at my campground and parked his rig next to mine. What I didn't mention at the time was that he had driven several tons of truck, fifth wheel, trailer (plus seven animals) 1,500 miles in three days - all to be here with me.

We met in an online forum dedicated to our mutual interest in sugar gliders. He started emailing me outside of the forum when I asked the group for advice about moving into an RV full time with gliders. Through our emails we found that we have a lot in common and we make each other laugh.

It wasn't long before we were talking on the phone and texting every day as he gave me emotional support through the stressful process of transitioning into the RV. My description of this mountain campground paradise, plus the strong connection between us, was too much for him to pass up. He packed up all his gear from the Arizona desert where he had been prospecting for gold and moved it all up here.

Romance bloomed right along with the Spring. We enjoy each other's company tremendously (even occasionally breaking into Monty Python sing-a-longs) and are quite simply comfortable with each other in a way that neither of us has ever experienced before. We come from different lives and different perspectives, but our choices have lead both of us here to this time and place together.

When the high season comes to an end here in Leavenworth, we'll head to another destination together. We don't know where that will be yet – offers of employment with site hookups will be happily considered! – but we know that we'll be traveling there together.

Our situation has the ideal balance of togetherness and solitude. We each maintain our own homes. We have our own beds, our own bathrooms, and our own kitchens. Nobody has to worry about picking up after the other, and nobody has to worry about offending the other's cleanliness standards. Nobody gets disappointed if the other needs to be alone for a while. We respect each other's time and space.

And yet we still get to play house. There is no stress or negotiation of trying to schedule dates! Since we're right next door, we can drop in for just a minute to say hi, or an hour to hang out. We can get together to chat over coffee/tea first thing in the morning. It's easy here to find time every day to focus on each other.

Course Change
Thursday, June 29, 2017

It was just over a year ago when I was temporarily dedicated to a community in Greece and found that the work required of me was more than I was able to give. I learned from that experience that I have to honor my own needs in order to be able to give back to others. I also learned that I can't do my best when I don't feel good – a simple concept, but a difficult boundary to hold in the face of pressing needs.

As much as I love this gorgeous mountain paradise where I've been planted since April, I recently found myself not feeling good about being here. Even though the atmosphere is ideal and the people are great... again, the work required is more than I'm willing to give.

I have so many potential projects bubbling in my cauldron of inspiration, just waiting to take shape in the world, but the majority of my energy is being devoted to the campground instead of to manifesting my visions. My vocation as an Inspired Dreamer compels me to change course - to follow my heart, and to pursue my passions.

Dave and I will soon be packing up to leave our short, but illustrious career as workampers. Instead, we'll be exploring the wonderful world of boondocking, which is the practice of RV camping without any hookups for power, water, or waste disposal.

Even though it takes a few lifestyle changes and behavioral fine tuning, our RV homes are designed to be fully functional off the grid. Dave has some experience in the lifestyle, having boondocked in the Arizona desert earlier this year, so that's an advantage.

Our first camp will be a remote location about an hour from where we are now. We asked for recommendations from fellow rockhounds for a good place to park RVs off road near our destination. After setting up our camp, then we'll be exploring the nearby geode beds. With his passion for treasure hunting and my love for rocks and gems, we're both really excited to start searching for some cool stones!

Without jobs consuming our time and attention, we'll be able to devote our energies to writing and getting our respective websites, blogs, videos, photos, and sales online and ready for the world.

I'm repeating the cycle of working up my courage to make another big leap. There was some illusion of security and continuity here in the campground for the summer, even though I knew I'd be moving on soon enough anyway. But now I'm filled with excited anxiety about yet another big change.

Breathe… Breathe…

My heart tells me it's time to move on. The universe has made it clear that this place has served its purpose for us, and that our continued adventures lie outside of these gates. I'm so very, very excited to continue this journey… but I recognize that my treasured bodily comforts are about to take a serious downgrading again. (Ah, the price of freedom.)

We have good capacity to hold water for washing and drinking, but it's not limitless. Daily showers will be a thing of the past. We'll have to be strategic when washing dishes. Toilet flushing will demand precision balance of enough water to prevent clogged pipes without wasting a limited resource.

Solar panels and gas-powered generators should be enough to cover our power needs, but waste disposal… that's really the "fun" part. I am now the proud owner of a 42-gallon tank on wheels. This will be used to drain our RV waste tanks, then be towed off somewhere that accepts such things for disposal. How often that unpleasant task needs to happen depends entirely on our behavior with water. (Talk about motivation for conservation.)

So the learning curve continues in an upward direction for me. Change is still a constant. Choices demand to be made. I keep retreating forward into adventures unknown…

The Next Big Leap
Sunday, July 09, 2017

I've already come a long way from the lifestyle I intended to leave behind. I no longer spend my time in a cubicle, giving my 110% every day in the never-ending quest to improve profits for shareholders. I no longer live in a condo, totally insulated from the natural world. I no longer avoid leaving home because joining the horde of impassable traffic is just too daunting to contemplate.

The choices I've made have already created profound changes in my life. I've traveled the world, gaining new experiences and perspectives. I've met amazing people who are living in ways I never imagined. I've opened my mind to intriguing possibilities... and then leapt into the unknown, following little more than vision and inspiration.

While some choices lead to immediate long-term change (like moving from my condo into an RV), other choices are just stepping stones along the path into the deeper unknown – like my choice to be a workamper at a large corporate-owned campground.

Even though I get to be outdoors frequently and far from the world of cubicle dwelling (both huge bonuses for me), I'm still impacted by the same big business shenanigans that inspired my escape from corporate servitude in the first place.

There is great value in trying something new, even when – perhaps especially when - you discover that a dream isn't everything you thought it would be. So maybe workamping isn't really my thing, but I've gained valuable knowledge and experience.

And working in the campground wasn't a bad choice by any means. I can't imagine any other setting where Dave and I would have had the opportunity to meet, work together, both be part of a community, and form the bond that we now enjoy. This unique experience has allowed us to develop an unexpected partnership, and to make the choice to Retreat Forward together. For that, I'm very grateful!

Preparations for our first big adventure together are now in full swing. After today we have three days of work left, then two more days to pack up and move our RVs to the new site. We're using this time to assure that our off-grid systems are functioning well and provisioning ourselves as necessary.

Off-Roading (Liberty, WA)
Wednesday, July 19, 2017

Our adventure today took us unintentionally off-roading across a mountain peak in my car. To be fair, this was really the first chance that my previously city-dwelling "sport utility vehicle" had to prove it's more rugged capabilities, and it performed honorably, but let me back up to where this story started...

The RVs are set up in this gorgeous mountain meadow with almost total privacy and we're loving it here – all except the deeply distressing condition of being unable to get a strong mobile internet connection. We're adrift in a sea of non-connectedness and getting twitchier by the hour with the compulsive need to google something... anything, quick!

So today we went out searching through federal BLM lands (free legal "dispersed camping") for a site large enough to accommodate both of our big rigs, with decent mobile reception. We scoured the rural roadsides for any promising off-shoots before detouring up what looked like a one-lane cattle road.

The road was paved, with plenty of opportunity to turn back, so we explored the narrow and winding path up the mountain. I was feeling a little skeptical about the possibility of maneuvering our big rigs around these narrow roads and tight curves, but the area was beautiful and so we pressed on.

To our great joy, a large level area presented itself shortly thereafter. What's more, the mobile coverage was great! We found our next camp.

Since we already knew that the narrow winding roads we came from wouldn't be comfortable in our RVs, and we heard rumor that the forest service roads led all the way over the mountain back to our camp in Liberty, we ventured forth in hopes of finding another way to bring our homes to this beautiful site.

We encountered a couple of travelers who assured us that we were on the right road to Liberty, and gave us the number of the forest road to follow. The road was paved and our outlook was sunny.

We kept following the road even as it became gravel, and then became dirt. We kept following the road, even across "potholes the size of Buicks!", as described by another motorist we met along the way.

I was feeling like we should turn around. Our outing had already taken longer than I expected and I had no idea where we were, but the semi-famous Lion Rock was only a short distance away and I wanted to visit while in the neighborhood.

By this time, the "road" was nothing more than a jumbled pile of pointy rocks lodged deep in the dirt, so we stopped the car and walked for a bit. Later, driving back to the well-traveled path, we found that it led to a dead end.

We backtracked the way we'd came, following each off-shoot road to see if that was the turn we missed before. In places the dirt road was so bad that we had to get out and examine the terrain to find the best approach through it. There were a few harrowing moments, but no real danger – other than to my poor car's suspension.

Eventually we found our way back to the intersection where the other travelers had told us the number of the forest road – only to find that was exactly the point where we had made our wrong turn. (D'oh!)

Following the correct forest road with high hopes it would lead us across the wilderness and back to our camp in Liberty, we set out on the narrow bumpy lane. It was far bumpier than either of us had expected, but the forest service thoughtfully put up a series of signs and arrows that assured us we were on the right path – most of the time.

Sometimes, the forest service left us hanging. We had quite a lot of uncertainty with too many options in between signs, and I kept leaning over to glance at the gas gauge with visions of being stuck on a mountainside overnight, lost on the forest service roads.

We persevered through the doubt and followed the road downwards whenever the option presented. Eventually that strategy led us to a gravel road, which turned into the back road off which our current camp is located. (How convenient!)

So we didn't achieve our objective. We still haven't found an accessible boondocking site with good mobile coverage, but we did have an unexpected adventure and I got a few great photos.

Boondocking
Monday, July 24, 2017

Boondocking is the practice of living in an RV with no connections to the usual services – no power, no water, and no sewer disposal. By contrast, living in an RV at a campground with utility hookups isn't that much different than living in a regular (on-grid) house or apartment - unlimited power and water are instantly available, with easy disposal of garbage and waste.

But when boondocking, it's very important to be mindful of resource consumption and waste production. Take cooking dinner as an example. Food prep doesn't involve much consumption - as long as I'm careful to use a very little water for washing, and to keep food garbage to a minimum since everything must be packed into town for disposal.

When it comes to heating food the propane stove top works well, but burns a lot of fuel for lengthy cooking. My electric kitchen appliances will run only with the gas-powered generator.

There's always the old standby of the campfire, but that requires wood for fuel - and lack of a burn ban in hot/dry summer conditions. Another consideration is how much washing up will be required after cooking. The more pots that I use, the more washing I do; the quicker my freshwater tank empties, and the quicker my waste water tank fills.

Every choice I make - from how long I run the generator to power my air conditioning on a 90+ degree day, to how much water I'll use with each flush of the toilet – is made with conscious calculation of consumption versus necessity and convenience. How much am I using, and how bad do I need/want it? Is there any better way to use less?

The goal is to extend our limited resources as long as possible, before we have to pack up and move the rigs back out into the world for refilling and draining. Living this way takes more time and effort to meet the simple needs of everyday life. Quick and easy are conveniences of the past – reminiscent of a lifestyle that required too much of our time focused in other directions.

216

Ongoing conscious effort is required to maintain the boondocking lifestyle. We each keep watch daily on our supplies of propane, gasoline, and water. Sunny days collect enough solar power to watch a movie, but accidentally leaving the TV on all night drains the battery by the morning.

Firing up the generator solves the power problem, but gasoline is also limited. I love a nice hot shower, but that requires propane and time for heating, plus moving a lot of waste water to the gray tank.

And in exchange for all of these mindful inconveniences, I get to sit peacefully and quietly in this gorgeous remote location - free from rent, free from crowds, and free from the usual bills and trappings of domesticated American life. Priceless!

Safe Passage (Snoqualmie Pass, WA)
Saturday, July 29, 2017

When I was traveling in foreign countries, I had a lot of anxiety each time I moved from place to place. No matter how well I researched each route and destination to help alleviate that anxiety, I couldn't help feeling it.

I had so many fears about what could go wrong, what I might not know, what I could have prepared for better if only I had known more in advance! It was always with a profound sense of relief (and at least a little surprise) that I arrived safe and in a timely manner to each destination around the world. I'm finding that the anxiety has returned as I brave the unknown in learning the ways of RV travel.

Yesterday was the first time that I had to hook up my "toad" (car towed behind the motorhome) without the assistance of someone more knowledgeable and experienced than myself. I read the manual and instructions more than once. I was given a tutorial months ago by the mechanic who installed the towing apparatus. I've seen it done and assisted before.

There was no logical reason to suspect that my actions to connect the toad were faulty or negligent in any way... and still my emotions went off the chart with fear and dread. I was convinced that I was a danger to myself and others, and appalled that I'm legally allowed to hit the road with no certified proof of knowing how to work this get-up.

But fear is my old friend by now. We've been through a lot together and I've learned to handle the fear by expressing it. No stoicism here!

I let forth a rant of my anguished anxieties. I stomped my feet, shook my hands, and dropped F-bombs until the crows in the nearby trees complained loudly about my vulgarity and flew away.

Having released all that tension (and recharged with a nice long hug from Dave), I was ready to get behind the wheel with reasonable certainty that my fears were not founded.

We managed to get off the boondock field and onto the two-lane mountain highway with no trouble. A truck stop in Ellensburg offered a convenient place to top up on gas and to take a quick breather before getting back on the road.

Merging can be stressful in a big rig with limited visibility and maneuvering capability, but the merge onto I-90 yesterday was painless. And the larger highway means at least two lanes in each direction, so I don't have to worry about holding up traffic while going my preferred ten mph under the speed limit.

Following a tip from a local RV park, we were able to drain our waste water tanks at a rest stop about halfway to our new site. Then, only two hours after leaving our site in Liberty, we pulled into the new camp that we had scouted out the previous day. We were joyous to find that nobody else had claimed the site in the meantime, and we quickly set up our camp in the flat circular clearing guarded by tall Douglas Firs in all directions.

The next challenge is finding nearby sources for water, fuel, food, and dumping. Remote areas are great for natural beauty, but not so good for conveniences. However, this new site of ours does come with strong mobile coverage, and we're now spending hours absorbed in updates, emails, downloads, and all of the other assorted business we put on hold while we were without access for more than two weeks.

So another passage has been successfully completed. We have campsites lined up through at least the middle of August after this one, giving us plenty of time to scout out our next adventure!

Progress
Monday, August 14, 2017

It was lovely to camp out in that quiet mountain meadow in Liberty, but I was in denial about the level of impact that the lack of internet access had on my productivity. Once we settled into our next location – with fast reliable mobile connectivity – I dove into my new planning project with wild abandon.

Armed with a fresh spreadsheet, I scoured the internet for reports of boondocking and "dispersed camping" sites, which is what the Forest Service calls the random clearings on federal land that aren't official campsites and don't offer any services. Google maps is also a handy tool because all park lands are indicated in green, so I just started looking for likely boondocking places in the big green spaces on the map.

To broaden our range of options, I also looked at locations closer to civilization. I'm not interested in sleeping in a WalMart parking lot (a popular short-term option among boondockers), but I found that it's common for casinos to offer RV parking at little or no cost for up to fourteen nights. Especially since the casinos around here tend to be in beautiful areas, that may be an appealing option!

But internet research can only take us so far, given that I'm not going to move this bus without knowing where I'm going to park it at the end of the day. Planning phase two is when we go out scouting on forest service roads to find a new secluded spot (with mobile coverage!) that can accommodate our two big rigs.

I've mapped out what I'm hoping will be a relatively smooth route into and out of the Olympic National Forest, crossing through on forest service roads. The roads I've chosen are categorized as "passable by passenger vehicles." Whether that includes passenger vehicles 40+ feet long remains to be seen, but that's why we scout in advance!

As we gain knowledge and experience in this lifestyle, we're building up a library of boondocking options. Eventually we won't need to scout since we'll just go back to those places that we know meet all our needs. But until then... we keep learning.

For now, we're at a small RV park in my hometown so that I could attend my annual family reunion in the area. After all that seclusion and solitude on the mountain, it's a little odd to be back among people, and living in a park with neighbors only a few feet away. But it's nice to be able to make a quick trip to just about any type of store without planning in advance and driving an hour each way to reach civilization.

We both agree that boondocking is our preferred lifestyle and Dave keeps making improvements to our systems. The portable waste disposal tank is working great, but getting it up onto the truck when it's full remains a two-person job, even with the ramp he built. Next solution on the list is a pulley.

The 50-gallon water tank that we use to collect water and refill our tanks works great, but the holding tanks in our RVs are each 100-gallon so that means multiple trips for a fill up. Next on the upgrade list is a water tank with twice the capacity and a more convenient shape to better fill our tanks and take up less space on the truck bed.

It feels good to have a plan. Whether or not anything on my spreadsheet actually comes to pass, I have the security of a plan ready-made if fate fails to offer us better options in the meantime. I call that progress!

Meet the Critters
Tuesday, September 12, 2017

I would like to formally introduce you to the furry joys of my days: Yoda and Winky. These tiny creatures have had such an impact on my life that I thought a little get-to-know the sugar gliders should be presented!

The handsome fellow on top is my boy Yoda. He's an adventurous explorer and has a talent for finding his way into trouble. In addition to the irresistible charisma possessed by every sugar glider, Yoda has a uniquely adorable characteristic – he sniffles and snorts constantly. The vet said his health is fine, he's just so curious that he sniffs absolutely everything he can get his nose into!

The winsome beauty below is my girl Winky. When she came to me as a young joey, she was so scared and "crabbing" (making a loud scary noise) at everything. She was obviously determined to convince me what a fearsome beast she was, so I named her Jabberwinky. She eventually mellowed as we built trust between us, and her name was suitably shortened. Winky is still a cautious soul, but she'll follow Yoda into his adventures after he shows her the way.

They sleep in a pouch all day and then wake up around 8pm to party like rock stars in their big cage all night. About an hour before daylight, I wake up to let them out of the cage for play time. I've found mornings to be best because their boundless energy starts to wane a little before sleep time.

I open the cage door and one after the other leaps onto me, clinging to my clothes with their Velcro-like claws. They don't stay still for more than a moment, then take off running all over me or leaping off to explore around the RV. If Energizer had known about sugar gliders, that bunny would have been out of a job. When gliders are awake, they are non-stop action and excitement!

Every surface is a potential landing pad for a leap, horizontal or vertical. It was Yoda who discovered that they have the power to walk on the RV ceiling, which is carpeted. They can jump a few inches straight up and grab on with their claws, then easily run laps around the ceiling, often stopping to cling with only two paws while hanging upside down to get a good view the room.

During the day when they're asleep in the pouch, we have "sleepovers." That's when I join them in the pouch - or at least my hand joins them, which is all of me that will fit. The sleepy gliders will grab onto my fingers, or curl themselves into my palm. Sometimes I feel a furry tail being woven between my knuckles. This is really the only time that they're still enough for cuddles, which makes it all the sweeter.

I keep well-stocked on sanitizing wipes because gliders aren't the sort to be potty trained. There is nothing in my home that hasn't been touched by something that comes out of a glider, but that's the price we pay for living with these critters. We suffer the tiny bites and the midnight barking fests ("let me sing you the song of my people..."), and wouldn't have it any other way.

The Boondocks (Sappho, WA)
Saturday, September 23, 2017

We are definitely in the boondocks now! Along an unpopulated stretch of rural highway, off a side street and down a gravel forest service road is the nearly hidden entrance to our secret valley in the forest. The driveway goes down and around a corner, leaving our large forest clearing completely invisible from the road. All I can see for 360 degrees is trees and sky. It's beautiful!

If you're not familiar with the term, "the boondocks" refers to remote places far from the comforts of civilization. Naturally, the practice of boondocking in an RV means going well beyond the outskirts of even the tiniest town. Without the usual services of civilization like grid power or water nearby, maintaining our own personal levels of comfort and convenience requires some off-grid systems.

Dave and I have been boondocking together in our RVs for just over two months, but it wasn't until we camped in the rain forest recently that I truly learned what it means to be unplugged. Up until then, I'd always been able to take advantage of the extra solar power generated by his RV. However, parking under the rainforest canopy means that the trees have first dibs on all the sunshine, and they're not sharing.

My rig has on-board batteries to keep things like lights and fans on when not plugged in, but that power only goes so far. My fridge consumes battery power and so does my furnace fan. I found myself with a dead battery and unable to start my generator on the first morning after a chilly night. (Dave to the rescue, of course!)

As Autumn settles in, the temperature here up north drops quickly. The choice most boondockers make is to head south, so we'll be following the annual migration of snowbirds to the milder climate in Arizona. Not only are the public lands flat, free, and plentiful for boondocking, but the town of Quartzsite, AZ hosts an annual trade-show for all things RV related, which draws tens of thousands of RVers to the area. (I hear that it's like Burning Man for retired folk.)

So we'll go to the desert and absorb all the knowledge and experience we can from the hordes of full-time boondockers. I need to learn more about solar power anyway, since running a gas generator wears on my conscience. I have no idea what other fancy tricks and toys the show might have to offer, but I'm eager to dive in and explore!

Civilization (Bremerton, WA)
Saturday, October 07, 2017

You may notice that this photo of the Seattle skyline is very different than my last location, boondocking out in the woods. The day after I posted my last blog from the comfort of our secret forest hideaway, I got a call that my dad was in the hospital, so we packed up and headed as close as we could get back to civilization the next day.

I'm happy to report that Dad is now back home, recovering from major surgery, and with a reasonably clean bill of health. My family always comes together in times of crisis, and this time was no different. Everybody pitched in to assure that Dad was exceptionally well taken care of at two different hospitals, and to assure that Mom had what she needed to stay by his side.

But moving to be near my family meant leaving my beloved woodsy solitude behind. The boondocking opportunities in town are limited to parking lots, which is not somewhere I want to be, and all the local RV parks are already full. This left us with a dilemma - no good place to park our homes nearby.

With our options limited, we chose a solution that's less than ideal. For the first time since we met, Dave and I are now miles apart instead of right next to each other. We're only about a ten-minute drive away, but the distance creates a definite shift in our lifestyle.

Enjoying our morning ritual of coffeetea together requires somebody to be alert enough to drive, instead of just stumbling out of bed and wandering next door. We have to make plans to spend time together instead of the usual spontaneous drop-ins.

Dave and I started out living together and now we've progressed on to dating. I think we might have read the relationship manual backwards!

The people I love are alive and well, happy and healthy. My mobile lifestyle gave me the flexibility to be with family as needed. Our plans to head south may be a little delayed, but we can take care of a lot of business while here in civilization.

Life is good and the adventure goes on!

Interlude
Sunday, October 22, 2017

Six months ago I began another adventure into the unknown, setting off into a steep learning curve as I embraced the lifestyle of a full time RVer. I've stayed in relatively familiar territory (my home state) while gaining the skills I need to safely move this bus from place to place and to maintain a comfortable home. Now that I have some minimal clue as to how it all works, it's time for me to turn this adventure up a notch!

After a month of sitting in my home town for family time and to take care of some business, we're now getting ready to hit the road for a long haul. On the road again! Wohoo!

My fears are suggesting that I must have surely forgotten how to drive this beast in the month I've been sitting still, but I'm sure that feeling will quickly fade once I'm actually in motion.

I've planned a leisurely six-day journey to Joshua Tree National Park in southern California, where we'll boondock for a week or two while getting a feel for the area. Our final destination is about a hundred miles east of there in the town of Quartzsite, Arizona – a desert mecca for us mobile types who are escaping from the harsher winter climates of more northern areas.

We should arrive in Quartzsite in early November, giving us plenty of time to stake out a claim on a site close to town, hopefully before tens of thousands of other RVers arrive to camp for the season. The town hosts an annual two-month long trade show focusing on everything RV-related and gems/minerals. (They might as well just send us an engraved invitation, since the whole show is tailored to our interests.)

I expect that we'll learn a lot from all the trade show folks selling the latest and greatest in off-grid technology. I've been thinking of getting my RV set up for solar power (a significant investment), and look forward to finding a great deal at the show after perusing the many options. Who knows what other temptations and innovations we'll find to make our lives on the road easier and more sustainable?

It's been great to be plugged into "shore power" while parked here in my home town. (I can run my heater and my toaster at the same time!) Having the flexibility to live near my parents during a difficult time was priceless. The convenience of being close to shops and services has been great, but I'm longing for the peace found only in more remote locations.

It's almost time for these wheels to start rolling again. I can't wait to get back to adventuring and telling y'all about it!

Day of Rest (Bakersfield, CA)
Tuesday, October 31, 2017

Last night marked the completion of Day 3 of our six-day journey southbound. Halfway there!

I tend to have a wee bit of anxiety about piloting this ground-craft, but after a few months of moving the rig around my home state I was feeling pretty good about taking the training wheels off, so to speak.

Before departure on Day 1, Mom made us a hearty breakfast and we enjoyed a warm sendoff from the hospitality of my parents' property. With the addition of walkie talkies to our equipment, Dave and I are now able to communicate safely and easily while driving, reducing my stress level even more. I was feeling nothing but eagerness to get on the road – no fear!

Our stops have gone according to plan and we haven't encountered any major issues. (Yet – knocking on wood.) All is well.

And still, my body shows signs of high stress. I never really feel like eating on passage days, too eager to get the moving part over so that I can relax the hyper-vigilance needed while driving. I end up very tired and hungry by the time we stop if I don't eat, so I try to force at least a little something into my system.

That works OK when I'm only driving for a few hours and staying for a few days, but I'm finding that my stamina for driving many consecutive hours and days is very limited.

On the third driving day of not eating or sleeping particularly well, and about to face a mountain, I woke up feeling that old familiar anxiety - that tightening in the gut and deep internal quiver that you can't quite make still.

Dave assured me that everything was fine and there was no challenge ahead that I couldn't face (or that he couldn't help me with.) I agreed, and chalked up my feelings to hormones or whatever. The passage was going smoothly and we had already stopped a couple of times for breaks. I had eaten a little lunch, but had to force it.

Then sometime in the afternoon, after the hardest part of the mountain was already behind us and there was nothing but easy road ahead of me... I found myself suddenly feeling on the verge of panic.

It's not that I thought something bad was going to happen – I could see quite clearly that my driving was fine and that the road was safe. There was no apparent trigger for the shaky, weak, teary-eyed, terrified feelings that suddenly overwhelmed me.

I called to Dave on the radio and we pulled over at the next exit. After safely parking our rigs, I got out to release all that pent-up nervous energy, then drank some juice and ate a couple handfuls of nuts. The shaking stopped and the fears faded back into tolerable levels.

OK, so it seems that I haven't been taking proper care of myself. Too little food, too little quality sleep, and too much intensity of focus while driving leaves my energy reserves too drained to cope with life.

So today we're staying put. We're at a friendly (free of charge) casino truck parking lot in sunny California, so we're just gonna sit right here today. I'm going to eat three reasonably balanced meals, take a walk, maybe take a nap, maybe give myself a pedicure. I don't know for sure, but it will be all about taking it easy to fill my depleted reserves.

We have one more long day of driving then two more shorter

days before arriving at Joshua Tree National Park. After this brief refresher (and more diligence in taking care of my own needs) we should continue enjoying a smooth ride southbound. On with the adventure!

Quartzsite - First Impressions (Quartzsite, AZ)
Saturday, November 11, 2017

Quartzsite is a tiny desert town in the southwest corner of Arizona. There are about 3,500 year-round residents and another million or so RVers who camp out seasonally on the abundant open flat land.

Resources like fresh water are available in town, but for fees that add up quickly over time. One dollar for five gallons sounds reasonable, until you're trying to fill a 100-gallon tank every couple of weeks. So instead of camping for free and paying for resources, we paid to camp in the official Long Term Visitor Area (LTVA).

The LTVA is about 11,000 acres that Arizona set aside for RVers to do their thing with minimal impact to the environment. There are stations with unlimited fresh water, trash dumpsters, and dump stations for draining waste tanks. There's a fee for camping in the LTVA, but at the rate of $180 total for up to six months, it's the cheapest rent I've ever paid.

We arrived in early November to find that thousands of desert-dwellers had already made camp, but we had no problem staking our claim on a piece of prime ground backed up to some rare trees and brush for privacy.

Although I haven't seen so much as a speck of trash, evidence of previous years' campers is everywhere. Rocks have been used to create private driveways, fire pits, and campsite boundaries around many areas. The spot we chose alongside a dry creek bed is already landscaped with little islands of bushes and debris surrounded by rocks. We'll be working to add a driveway and our own personal touches to the outdoor décor as soon as we become more accustomed to all this sunshine.

The entrepreneurial spirit is strong in Quartzsite. It's not the profit-driven mindset that's found in big business, but rather the simple independent will to survive. It's the retired guy living in his trailer, offering barber services in his tent outside. It's the folks selling recently expired packaged foods for awesome prices from a big tent in a parking lot. It's the flea market, where some residents both live and make a living buying and selling old used stuff every day.

There isn't any one-stop shopping in this town, although most shops have an interesting variety of things you might need. Aside from the expired food tents, there are three brick and mortar stores selling food. (You can also buy guns and ammo at one of them.) One store has good meat, one store has OK produce, and none of them have good sourdough bread. (Bummer.)

The people here have all been welcoming and informative. Pretty much everybody is happy to strike up a conversation, and strangers smile and wave as they pass each other in the LTVA. There are still six weeks until the big tent show starts in January and this valley is going to fill up with a big crowd of interesting folks.

I understand that Arizona tends to be a very politically conservative region, but I'm sure that we'll all get along if we just avoid the usual hot topics. However, as I was wandered the flea market today, I found something disturbing. It was a sign for sale that read: *No Dogs, No Negros, No Mexicans.*

That's not cool. I don't know if it was vintage or meant to be funny, but it stopped me in my tracks. Who buys a sign like that? Who sells one?

The sign was a reminder that I'm no longer in the progressive bastion of the Pacific Northwest. I can't imagine seeing something like that sign for sale in Seattle without a crowd of people making a stink about it, but here... no big deal.

Other than that, I'm really enjoying it here. We're still learning how to mitigate the harsh desert sun, but with the addition of a large heat shield to my front window, and an even larger shade net hung in the path of the afternoon sun, my home is staying much more comfortable.

The sunrises, sunsets, stars at night, and distant mountains protecting this huge desert cauldron fill my senses with the beauty of nature in every minute. This place feels abundant and inspiring to me. I can't wait to see what happens next!

Rockin' in the Free World
Thursday, November 23, 2017

My homeland of the Pacific Northwest is teeming with lush greenery due to the frequent rainfall, but this comparatively stark Southwest desert is filled with beauty of its own.

I can't stop looking down at the gravel everywhere I go, especial-ly since I found this beautiful quartz crystal! When I can manage to tear my eyes away from the little rocks on the ground to glance up at the horizon, my gaze is greeted by rugged peaks of bigger and bigger rocks, finally grown into mountains in the distance.

The abundance of interesting rocks in the environment appears to be inspirational and I'm certainly not immune to their effects. I've been spending time nearly every day hauling and arranging rocks to make an attractive border around our camp. (OK, so maybe I'm marking my territory, but I want it to look pretty too!)

Many other campsites have been marked with rock borders as well, and it's not uncommon to find rock art in many forms. Rocks are a passion and a way of life around here, with many vendors in town selling huge bins of more types of rough gems than you can imagine. (Honestly, it's enough to make a poor rockhound drool.)

We recently joined the Quartzsite Roadrunner Gem and Mineral Club, which seems to be the hottest ticket in town. The clubhouse is more of a campus, with several buildings needed to hold the equipment for many different specializations: lapidary, opal cutting, faceting, flint knapping, leather work, steel work, silver smithing, casting, and more.

And like I said, this club is hoppin'. They also host dinners, dances, and fundraisers. They have rockhounding field trips and ATV group treks into the desert. They operate most workshops on the campus for two 3-hour shifts every day – completely run by volunteers.

Not only do we now have access to professional level tools to learn on, but also a wealth of classes and instructors to help guide us into competency in several areas. Oh yea. We're gonna soak up these skills until there's no more to learn!

We took our own field trip to Crystal Hill yesterday, climbing a small mountain of shale to find veins of quartz and washes of quartz chunks. The climb wasn't too strenuous and we were having a great time finding big deposits, but the sun drove us back to shelter before we were really ready to stop hunting.

So while I do miss the cool damp shade of the evergreens back home, I'm in awe of the earthy beauty surrounding me in this very different place. The sun is relentless, but I have shelter and air conditioning when I really need it.

The twilight times here are magical – in the cold of morning when the golden glow of sun just begins dusting the edge of the mountains, and in the fading light of day as the horizon sets on fire with streaks of magenta and violet. There is no event to compare to the sun making his entrance and exit over the desert each day.

Our campsite still feels private and secluded, but we see more RVs arriving every day. I hear that there's a big influx of new rigs expected to arrive after Thanksgiving – which is tomorrow. I'm hoping that my rock border will deter newcomers from parking too close, but it's literally the wild west out here and there's no rules, so we'll see…

Dental Tourism
Friday, November 24, 2017

The small Mexican town of Los Algodones is a thriving center of medical tourism for Americans. I never expected to cross the border in search of care, but that was before Dave's toothache became unbearable and we had to explore some options.

Forty minutes north of us is a dentist in Arizona whose next open appointment is three weeks away at a cost of $325 per extraction. Only ninety minutes south of us is the Mexican border and the mecca of dental tourism in this region – with an average cost of $50 for that exact same extraction. (That's only 15% of the American price, for anybody who's keeping track.)

Making the same-day appointment with the dentist in Mexico was quick and painless, and we were at the border shortly before Dave's 11am time slot. We paid a small fee to park in the large secure parking lot on the US side, then walked two blocks into Mexico to the clinic.

Before we could even get out of the parking lot there were street hawkers calling out for dental and optical services, as well as jewelry and souvenirs. It was surreal to be accosted every few feet by someone wearing scrubs asking if we needed a dentist.

The clinic itself was an oasis of peace beyond the chaos of the sidewalks. It had a small, very white waiting room behind the bright green door of its entrance. One couch was positioned to view the flat screen TV (showing Mexican soap operas, of course) mounted over the reception desk. One small restroom completed the waiting area.

About thirty minutes after the appointment time, Dave was escorted back to one of four small treatment rooms, very clean with all modern equipment. The dentist spoke perfect English and I'm told that she was very skilled in her work.

I went out to explore the town and find some lunch while he got the work done. The scent of carne asada wafting on the breeeze summoned me to the corner shop where meat was grilling over an open flame. Two tacos and one cerveza later, my belly was full and I returned to the clinic to collect Dave and his gauze-stuffed cheek.

With a couple of molars in his pocket, Dave and I left the clinic in search of the farmacia to collect the antibiotics and pain meds he was prescribed. The waiting line to cross back into the US on foot was about 20 minutes, and then we were on our way back home.

The quality of care he received was as good or better than any we've received in the US. The ease of making an appointment, and the outrageously low cost in comparison, show that it's entirely possible to operate a thriving and affordable healthcare industry - contrary to the example of the US system. I'm grateful that we have this option so close to our temporary home!

Moving Forward
Wednesday, December 06, 2017

I'm not currently employed. My time and energy aren't currently spent producing income. By some standards, my life is going nowhere fast. So it's a good thing that I have my own standards, because by my own measure I'm moving forward at a steady pace!

Five years ago I was overstressed and dissatisfied with my lifestyle. I had a well-paying job and a home conveniently located near the city. I was active in my community and had plenty of friends and family nearby. I had the luxury to eat out whenever I wanted and to indulge in occasional frivolous purchases. By most common measures, my life was a success.

My time was spent focused on the rigors of a standard work

week, leaving me only weekends to tend to the business of life while trying to squeeze in desperately needed rest and relaxation as well. And though my allotted three weeks of vacation per year was generous by American standards, it wasn't nearly enough time to pursue any dream that took me away from home.

I took a hard look at my circumstances and decided that I needed to make significant changes if I wanted to grow into the better life that I envisioned for myself. There were years of planning, saving, and paying off debt before I finally made the blind leap into the unknown – quitting my job, leaving my home, and setting off into the wide world to meet whatever adventure might find me.

There are so many clichés about lost wanderers, finding yourself through travel, and finding yourself after returning home. And it's true – new experiences and new perspectives are indeed revealing and transformative. But like Forest Gump with his box of choco-lates, you never know what you're going to get when you travel.

I never dreamed that I would stumble into off-grid living through buying a used RV, getting a minimum wage job in a campground, meeting an amazing partner, and leaving that job to set off into rent-free adventures on remote public lands. (Honestly, did you see that coming?) My life has taken a number of unexpected turns, but I'm still headed in the direction I want to be going.

Among the unexpected turns is a dear friend who recently decid-ed that she loves my former home enough to make it her own. The sale of the condo formerly known as mine officially closes today. My gratitude goes out to Jen and the universe at large for facilitat-ing such a huge, but painless step forward!

I think this officially makes me a vagabond. I own nothing but what I carry with me. The open road is my address.

That's all poetic and stuff... up until I want to receive a delivery. Or register to vote. Or sit still for a while. So our next step is to estab-lish a home base in Washington state, within an hour of my family.

At long, long last... I'll finally achieve my dearest wish of taking stewardship for ("owning") my own little piece of the Earth. With

236

the proceeds from the condo sale, I can afford a few remote acres where our RVs can sit peacefully among wilderness and greenery. Ah… bliss.

Once the home base is established, then I can go about the business of becoming a productive citizen again. We'll dig literal roots into the ground (I dream of an orchard as well as a veggie garden), and figurative roots into our chosen community.

Our homes will still have wheels and our spirits will still be filled with adventure, so our travels will of course continue. We'll just have a home to come back to, near enough to share with family and friends.

I had no idea how I would come to this point and I am so excited to keep moving forward into the unknown!

Whirlwind!
Tuesday, December 12, 2017

One week ago I mentioned a desire to purchase land at some point in the future. Well, patience has never been my strongest virtue and "carpe diem" has really been working for me lately, so... I just submitted an official Offer to Purchase a nice chunk of land on the Olympic Peninsula overlooking Hood Canal.

My plan was to wait until I was back in the Pacific Northwest to view a bunch of properties and find just the right one, but I can't resist scanning the real estate listings now anyway. And then a property that so perfectly meets my needs appeared that I was compelled to take decisive action. It even has two full hookups for RVs already installed, so it's totally "move-in-ready!"

I spent the last four days flying between Phoenix and Seattle, viewing and hiking the semi-remote and definitely rugged property, and spending one night apiece with each of three households of my immediate family. (I won't be "home for the holidays" this year, so this quick visit was my substitute.) I'm exhausted, but exhilarated!

Google has been an awesome research assistant as I obsessively sleuthed out every bit of information I could find about this property. I was able to confirm that all systems (grid power, capped spring for water, and septic) were professionally designed and installed, and that the land has been permitted as a build site in the past.

After all that research, I feel confident that the property is a sound investment and should serve me well in the future. All signs point to go! So with baited breath… I submitted my formal offer.

My offer is lower than the asking price, but I'm hoping that their unusual circumstances and my somewhat poetic plea to allow me to take stewardship of the land may sway the sellers into accepting.

It's possible that they could accept my offer, low as it is. It's possible that my long term dream – having my very own little piece of earth and trees – may become reality in the very near future.

People talk about following your bliss and all that, but I never expected that my bliss would lead the universe to just lay something like this at my feet. The sellers have until the end of this week to respond to my offer, so we'll see soon enough if this wild magic is for real…

Waiting
Sunday, January 28, 2018

Change your life! Try something completely different! It'll be new and exciting!

Um, yea. It will also be something you've never done before, don't know how to do, and will likely mean bumbling your way through while making big messy mistakes left and right. Sounds like fun, right? (Unless you happen to be something of a perfectionist like me, in which case it will all be mildly excruciating as well.)

Ever since I started this journey away from everything familiar I've been on one steep learning curve after another. I've traveled in unfamiliar countries with foreign languages, currencies, and cultural expectations. I've faced the fear of learning to drive a "big rig" and hauled all my worldly possessions 1,300 miles to an unfamiliar destination. I'm learning how to be and have a life partner after more than twenty years of living on my own.

And now I'm facing the thrilling and terrifying prospect of land ownership. My first offer for the RV-ready acreage on a hillside was rejected when they received a full price offer on the same day. OK, so that wasn't meant to be, but that just means that I get to keep looking!

My fickle heart fell in love with another contender without delay and I just submitted another Offer to Purchase an amazingly beautiful parcel of raw mostly forested land.

Raw land means that all the decisions around installing electricity, water well, septic system, broadband access, where to put buildings, etc. are all on me. I'll definitely get professional advice and assistance with all of that, but that still involves a level of knowledge I don't have in choosing the right professionals to do the jobs well.

I want this. I mean, I *really* want this. Living back among the quiet solitude of trees has been my dream ever since I moved away from the forest of my childhood. I've done so much research on this property and on the County regulations for using it. I read the Purchase Agreement in detail three times before signing. My due diligence is done.

I'm 99% confident that everything will work out fine if my offer to purchase is accepted... and yet my emotions are running wild. I'm on the verge of tears, I'm poised to snap in irritation, and I just can't get comfortable inside or out. I'm a mess of anxiety.

Much like a woman awaiting the results of her first pregnancy test, I'm waiting to hear if this is when everything changes. I'm waiting to hear if the next phase of my journey starts here and now. I'm waiting to hear if this is the opportunity into which I'll pour all my creative energies, bringing something new into being in the world.

Or will it be just a moment of crushing disappointment before rallying my emotions for another try? I don't know. And so I wait...

I got it!
Wednesday, January 31, 2018

I am nearly a landowner! Only two months of escrow to wait, and then that little chunk of paradise is all mine – with all the rights and responsibilities thereof. Woohoo!!

As mentioned in my last post, I did a lot of research and vetting before making my offer to purchase. What I didn't mention is... I haven't actually been to the land in person yet.

Yea, I know that's crazy. I just plunked down my life savings for land I've never set foot on.

Those ten acres of woodland that I grew up on were shared with my parents and sisters. They all know exactly the environment that I'm longing to return to and so I was able to trust their judgment completely when they visited the property and confirmed it has everything I want. Thus, I made one of the biggest decisions of my life based on faith... and research. Lots of research.

Now I begin the process of confirming feasibility – determining if the land can be made livable with services like a water well, septic system, and high-speed internet. (Let's be honest, a strong internet connection is at least as important as flushing the toilet.)

This is also the part when I learn how much all of this is going to cost and how much I may or may not have leftover for little luxuries like putting gravel down over muddy spots.

The good news is that sitting in one spot for a while should allow me to find gainful employment again and hopefully start replenishing my severely abused savings account. If anybody is in need of a ridiculously organized planner with a great attitude towards life and recent construction project management experience... let me know!

I was able to negotiate for us to occupy the property a few weeks prior to the official closing date so I'm excited to announce that we'll be returning to the Northwest in mid-March! We'll be working like mad immediately to line up installation of services on the property and then we'll be free to let our creative processes run wild while we do our best to improve on paradise.

The learning curve is ramping up again and my emotional volatility is following suit. The pendulum of my mood is swinging wildly from elation to irritation and back again. I'm excited, scared, unsure, ready to tackle the world... I have all the feels.

I also have a wonderful partner who's learning to deal with my mood swings. No matter how hard I try not to let my pendulum smack him upside the head, it's hard to avoid collateral damage when a volcano suddenly erupts nearby.

I'm reminding myself to enjoy the last of our time here in Quartzsite, but the compulsion to head north is strong. It's not time to go yet. We still have goals and social plans to meet before reversing our southern migration.

My body is still here in the desert, but my mind has already departed for the property and my spirit is pulling as hard as she can to make haste towards the trees...

Preparations
Saturday, February 17, 2018

Four months in the southwest is long enough to hide from the harsh northern winter and so preparations are in full swing for our imminent return to the Pacific Northwest. In between bouts of obsessively researching, planning and budgeting for my land development project, I've also been plotting a course home.

As the estimates to install utilities at my new property slowly come rolling in, while many more development necessities make themselves known, my budget looks slimmer and slimmer. I keep stressing to find creative ways to stretch my budget to achieve everything we need.

But then I remind myself... we're boondockers. All we actually NEED is a flat piece of land - and we've got that!

There's plenty of time to earn more money and build slowly. With a state park only two miles away that offers an RV dump station and potable water source, our long term needs are met. We're fully equipped to generate our own power and our mobile internet works well in the area. Whether we install utilities to the property now or later, we're still living in comfort.

I'm grateful that every member of my family has already visited my new homesite and provided me with photos and videos. Dave and I haven't even set foot on the property yet, but already our creative visions are flowing. I can't even imagine what inspiration we'll come up with once we're actually on the land!

It's still a couple weeks until we pull up stakes and hit the road, so we're using that time make sure our rigs are in top shape for travel. Dave has new tires and I have newly cleaned holding tanks. Oil is changed, pressure is checked - all systems tested and ready. There's plenty to do and yet the days can't seem to pass by fast enough.

We've been sitting still too long and the urge to get moving is growing by the day... especially because this time, our new home is waiting!

Dreams and Visions
Tuesday, February 27, 2018

This whole adventure began with a dream. I dreamed of spending more time experiencing the awe-inspiring beauty of our planet, and less time feeling stressed. Of course, that's a pretty broad goal with a lot of ways it could be achieved.

So how do you pick just one direction in life, once you've realized that the options are nearly limitless...?

Have you ever heard the phrase, "paralyzed by choice?" I moved past that paralyzed state by (metaphorically) throwing myself off a cliff and simply trusting the winds of fate to carry me to the place where I didn't know that I'd always wanted to go.

I left my career, my home, my friends and family, and flung myself out into the big wide world to connect with opportunities unknown. I decided to make the most of my travels by visiting places and people who were living as I hoped to live someday – sustainably with the environment and cooperatively within a community.

For years I had dreamed of living in an intentional community and so I took the opportunity to try that lifestyle with a few different groups. The people I met were all amazing individuals and those communities are doing some really remarkable things, but I discovered that I need more solitude than a full-time live-in community realistically allows.

And so I've honed my dreams with each new experience, finding what feels right and what doesn't really fit who and what I am. My desire to live and work cooperatively on projects of sustainability and creativity is still strong, but now I know that I'm happiest with the sanctuary of my own private space, and with only a few people nearby.

My impending purchase of undeveloped property fulfills the immediate need of a place to park our RVs in the region of my family, but it's also so much more. This property is the canvas upon which we'll bring our visions to life.

From this material of incredible raw natural beauty, we will shape and refine a Refuge from the stress-inducing environments of modern life. Far from the city, far from the traffic and the noise, far from the incessant demands of civilization – an oasis of peace and calm brimming with the restorative powers of nature, enabling rejuvenation of consciousness and creativity.

We have visions of a pond and waterfall, permaculture gardens, a secluded grove of tall trees, a heated outdoor shower, a huge brick oven/fireplace for cooking and gatherings, a big sheltered space filled with the tools to bring our dreams into life, and much more.

Although my vision is all focused on my plot of trees up north, my body is still here in the desert. We're packing up and taking care of business over the next few days before heading up to the Valley of Fire outside of Las Vegas to visit with friends for another few days.

After that, it's full steam ahead as we haul ourselves and all our worldly possessions up and down the mountains once again.

Homeward bound!

PART FIVE:

THE REFUGE

Life 2.0
Thursday, March 15, 2018

Five years ago, I decided that I wanted to change my life. I stretched my imagination as far open as it could go and began dreaming of possibilities beyond the life I had always known. For years, all my time and efforts (outside of my day job) were devoted to research, planning, and saving in order to achieve my vague, but oh-so-enticing dreams.

Then I took a leap – a big one – in leaving my career (and sole source of income) to follow my dreams. Everything inside me confirmed that I was making the right choice. I honestly didn't know where I'd end up, but I felt absolutely compelled to take that first step into the unknown.

Two years after that leap, I'm writing this blog from my awesome little tiny home on wheels, which is sitting in a clearing of native trees dripping with moss while birds sing from their perches up in the canopy.

This is my life now. Surrounded by the peace of nature, ensconced in my beloved comforts and conveniences with my wonderful partner in his own tiny home just a few meters away. Life is good!

However, that is not to say that everything is now all rainbows and unicorns in the happily ever after. This isn't that kind of story. The next chapter begins with more hard work and yet another steep learning curve, rife with frustrations and head-banging-against-the-wall type problems to solve.

Transforming this chunk of raw, muddy, wild, unpredictable Earth into a liveable homestead is our new challenge.

How? I don't know.

Scared? Oh, yea.

Upon Arrival...
Sunday, March 25, 2018

Getting settled on the new property was a lot harder than I anticipated and it's taken me some time to process before telling the story...

Our northern migration was completed without incident or accident, and we were feeling pretty confident as we drove the final miles onto the peninsula that is our new home. We decided to forgo our usual precaution of parking the RVs and checking out the property with my car first, and instead just drive straight onto the property with the rigs.

What could possibly go wrong? (Cue the ominous music.)

Driving my 36' motorhome with my car towed behind, I made the left turn onto the upward-sloped dirt driveway of our new home. Then my back tires started to sink into the soft wet sand at the entrance and I found that my rear bumper, along with the tow hitch for my car, were now buried together in the driveway.

Thanks to the marvel of the automatic leveling jacks on my RV (with gratitude to my Dad for insisting that I get that feature), we easily lifted the back out of the quicksand and Dave used brute force to de-couple the tow hitch, freeing my car. With just a bit more tire spinning in the mud, my RV then pulled itself up the driveway and onto a rare strip of relatively dry, level land.

Then came Dave's turn to tackle the driveway, with his monster truck towing a heavy 41' fifth wheel trailer. It took about an 18-point turn, but he managed to maneuver his rig into the driveway, where the rear end promptly sank into the sand and refused to go either forward or back.

He was stuck good. And he was completely blocking the only entrance and exit to the property.

For hours we tried to free his wheels and get some traction, only barely missing tipping the whole RV over an embankment. Nothing was working.

He carries a motorcycle in the garage of his rig and was able to open the garage ramp to get it out, so we rode into town to find some assistance. But after explaining our situation, even the local tow company said that there was nothing they could do if the entrance was blocked.

Back to the property we went, trying to come up with some creative solution. In desperation, we decided that the only option remaining to us was trying to use the powerful engine on my RV to help pull his rig onto firmer ground.

We carefully started backing my RV down toward Dave's, which is when mine got stuck in the mud as well. Both rigs were now immobilized.

We had been making quite a bit of racket with engines revving and wheels spinning, so I wasn't surprised to see a neighbor wander over to investigate. She asked if we could use a come-along and I agreed.

Our new neighbors avoided the blocked entrance by off-roading over the trail connecting our properties with their souped-up jeep sporting a big ol' winch with heavy-duty chains. (Cue the hero theme music!)

With the chains wrapped around my front axle and the jeep anchored to a nearby stump, it didn't take long to free my RV from the muck. When my home was back on dry ground, the guys went to work on the harder problem.

They toiled well past dark, trying various anchor points to get just the right angle to assist Dave's truck wheels to a point that they could pull his rig again. And at long last he was on level ground, but still hadn't cleared the driveway. A large cedar stump was perfectly placed to prevent his rig from completing the turn.

It took one more day, two chainsaws, and much more help from the neighbors to get Dave's rig out of the driveway, but eventually the exit was clear.

OK, so the property needs some work.

Drainage is a top priority, as is leveling the big clearing to be friendlier to our rigs. It wasn't quite as "move-in ready" as I hoped, but our homes are safe and warm... and now firmly planted where they're at until the swamp recedes.

Meeting Jack
Tuesday, April 03, 2018

I would like to formally state for the record that I don't know Jack. (In other words, I know nothing.)

I don't know anything about connecting to the electrical grid, nor anything about how water gets from underground into my nice convenient tap. I don't know anything about septic systems or how they interact with power and water. I don't anything about developing raw land into a habitable home, but I'm learning.

I'm the kind of person who likes to feel competent and in control. (Don't we all?) I like to have a deep understanding of whatever I'm working on so that I can avoid standard pitfalls.

But since Jack and I have yet to become acquainted, I'm basically flying blind. I don't even have the knowledge to recognize what's in front of my face, let alone anticipate what's coming. Wow, is that an uncomfortable place to be.

Thankfully, my new community is well-networked with exactly the kind of professionals who have the knowledge and experience that I lack. (Hello, Jack!) And as is common in small communities, each contractor I'm working with knows each of the other contractors personally and they're all accustomed to working together.

As the estimates to install services roll in, my immediate vision for the property is being narrowed into a laser focus: power, water, septic. That's all I can see now. Gardens, landscaping, garage, guest bathroom... all these things are luxuries to be built in the future as we gather more resources.

For now, we'll be lucky to stretch the budget far enough to cover the bare necessities. The reality of limited self-funding has finally arrived after these seemingly endless months of low-spend living, which extended my savings far longer than I ever thought possible. It's been a little over two years since I last earned a substantial paycheck, so I guess I'm overdue to start feeling the pinch.

Now I'm learning to be my own general contractor and looking for ways to continue supporting my dreams financially without going back to the world of cubicles and shareholders.

I'm excited and delighted, anxious and unsure, inspired with visions and petrified with fears. The plain truth is that I have NO IDEA what I'm doing, but still...

One decision at a time, The Refuge is taking shape.

One action at a time, we lay the foundation to support our dreams.

One day at a time, we slowly but surely keep moving forward.

The Grove
Wednesday, April 11, 2018

While waiting for all the contractors to align so that the big work can get started on the property, I'm jumping into my first DIY project – The Grove.

The first time I walked into this amazing circle of grand old cedars, towering firs, and moss-covered maples, I was struck by the beauty of the space. At the time, I was also struck by a lot of sticker vines and springy branches in my face since the area had obviously been growing wild for decades. My feet sunk into several inches of decaying leaves and rotting wood with each tentative step.

I haven't been carrying any garden tools in my motorhome, so to get started I collected some old tools from my Dad. I really like the feel of using these antique, but still totally sturdy, tools that my grandfather used before I was born. They're not shiny, but they get the job done!

Starting at the surface of the forest debris, I cleared away the leaf-layer with a rake. Under the leaves were a lot of logs and branches so rotten that they fell apart as I moved them. When the forest floor was finally visible, it revealed many big clumps of fern roots that didn't want to give up, along with at least a few dozen slim alder saplings taking up most of the space.

The next tool on the job was a large pickaxe, which did wonders for removing those fern roots. However, it did not do wonders for my back, shoulders, and knee.

My body isn't conditioned to physical labor yet, so I'm trying to take it easy as I ramp up my efforts. I can reasonably work for about an hour at a time, then work for another hour later the same day after a rest. That'll have to do for now... at least until everything stops hurting.

Fortunately, the weather lately has been providing a lot of opportunity to rest while it pours down rain and makes new little streamlets across the property. So like any good Pacific Northwesterner, I'm learning how to take advantage of the few minutes of dry that we get at a time during spring. And little by little, I'm making progress.

I want to be respectful of the native flora and fauna of the grove, but I also want to use the space and so some of the abundant plant life has to go. I ruthlessly ripped out every sticker vine I encountered (they'll be back to battle another day), but the alder saplings gave me pause.

I love trees. I don't want to kill trees... but there's just too many.

I approached the first sacrificial sapling and gave it a moment of my attention along with gratitude for its existence before making my apology and laying into it with a saw. With the slender trunk out of the way, I reached down to reveal more of the root... only to find that it wasn't a root at all.

What I thought were many individual trees were actually just vertical off-shoots from long winding branches that had been buried in the leafy debris. Upon realizing that I wasn't going to kill any trees after all, only tame a few branches gone wild, I felt much better.

Mud and Stress
Saturday, April 14, 2018

Mama told me there'd be days like this. Actually, what she said was more like, "You're going to have some challenges with that property", but Van Morrison is just a little more poetic.

Reality keeps interfering with my beautiful plans for smooth and easy development of this land. "Low budget" was also part of my plan and reality is definitely messing with me on that front. I keep reducing my expectations of what I can accomplish with my limited budget and now I'm down to postponing necessities.

Between fees to the light company to install a transformer and fees to an electrician to wire accessible outlets for our RVs, more than half of my budget will be consumed just for power - and that's the least expensive of the big three necessities (power, water, septic.)

My parents have generously offered to pay for digging the well as a "pre-inheritance" gift (thanks Mom and Dad!), but that still leaves the septic system looming as the largest expense. And on top of everything else in the budget, there's the need to do something about the soggy boggy condition of the land.

It's been raining nearly non-stop for the last week and I fear that our mud-ravaged driveway could soon become impassable. The driveway needs leveling and gravel asap, but the electric installation (in 4 - 8 weeks) may involve tearing up some of that ground, so waiting is the best option to avoid wasting money and efforts.

Every time another contractor gives me unwelcome news or estimates well beyond my expectations, I take it like the professional that I am. In the back of my mind I'm running panicked calculations and striking more items off my wish list, but on the outside I just smile and clarify, "was that $15,000 that you said?"

I think there might have been a few too many of those emotionally repressed moments lately because I've started feeling edgy and irritable. I've already learned on this journey that I need to vent my feelings as they happen or pay a price later. It seems that the cost of me being a pro in the face of land development stress is getting weepy in the supermarket later because I can't figure out what to eat for dinner.

The problem is that I haven't learned yet how to express myself authentically during a stressful situation without... shall we say... losing my shit. Nobody who's just trying to do their job should be subjected to that much authenticity from me. (Stand back! She's gonna blow!)

I was trained to present the standard social veneer – the calm, polite, polished demeanor expected between respectable people conducting business. And so I just keep calm and carry on, as the British say. Then I have a good cry and go in search of junk food.

My home is warm and dry (mostly), my vehicle gets me where I need to go, and all my needs are met. I'm living my dreams and making progress on a steady basis. What is there to stress about? (Other than money, but let's not talk about that.)

I just need to chill and let this adventure unfold like all of my others. And remind myself to breathe…

Irons in the Fire
Wednesday, May 02, 2018

With the return of the sun and the long-awaited onset of Spring, things are looking up! We've got the ball rolling (in several directions at once) and we're making progress on developing the property. The community continues to be very welcoming and we continue making valuable connections with the locals.

The first step towards getting grid power to the property has been completed with the installation of a shiny new transformer. There are many (many) more steps to go before we can flip the switch and plug in our rigs, but progress is progress!

Now we wait for the excavator to get us on his schedule so that this place can get flattened out and more accommodating to moving our big rigs around. Once the clearing is level, then we can tear up the ground again, digging trenches for the electrical and internet wiring.

And finally, we'll spread a few tons of gravel around for drainage and traction. At that point, we can finally invite guests to visit without fear of getting them stuck in the muck.

We're starting to collect building materials to construct the utility shed we'll need to house the electrical stuff and we're recruiting skilled labor from my family to help us get it done right. (Thanks, Scott and Susie!) I've got all the contractors on speed dial by now and I'm hoping that we'll have the basics of a livable homesite by mid-summer.

In other news, I'm currently in the testing and interview process for a local full-time job. It comes with great benefits and would give me lots of opportunity to connect more with the community. The job requires some level of confidentiality so I won't mention any specifics yet, but if all continues to go well... I could be starting work in June!

Dave's been keeping busy working for a couple of local homeowners who need help on a variety of projects from sanding the bottom of a boat to ripping invasive ivy from trees. These jobs are more challenging than any gym workout and his strength and stamina are improving at a quick pace. My conditioning is coming along more slowly as I continue waging battles against the underbrush around the property.

We've decided that, aside from making the property livable, our first big homesteading project will be beekeeping. Dave has been obsessively researching hives, equipment, and bee husbandry techniques for weeks. We even took a field trip to attend demonstrations at a bee farm to learn more about transferring a swarm into a hive.

Dave created a GoFundMe campaign to get started with a few hives and every supporter who donates as little as $20 gets one pound of fresh local honey as soon as the hives start producing.

Little by little, we're taking the steps that lead to the future we envision. The Refuge is beginning to manifest before our very eyes...

Win Some, Lose Some
Wednesday, May 16, 2018

In my experience, workplaces tend to be a lot like family. You have people in authority and those who are expected to toe the line, while everybody has different personality types and agendas and they're all just trying to get along without any major incidents. The success of any given family or work group largely depends on how well everybody interacts with each other.

I interviewed well and my test scores were great, but the job I was hoping for went to another candidate. When it came down to it, the final interview was to determine how each of three qualified candidates would fit with the manager and culture of the workplace.

Although I'm disappointed that I wasn't chosen, I'm also grateful that I won't be struggling to fit in with a group that's on a different wavelength than me.

So that's back to the drawing board for the income portion of the sustainable lifestyle I'm trying to build. Minor setback. Moving forward!

The donations that Dave has received so far from his GoFundMe campaign enabled him to purchase a used bee hive off Craigslist, which is even better than a new hive since it's already fully drawn out. The former occupants of the hive already built the wax combs inside, saving the next occupants that work so they can get right to producing honey.

It's late in the beekeeping season and Dave wasn't sure where he was going to be able to find a queen bee and her attendants for sale. But the empty hive was sitting on his back porch for less than 24 hours when he started noticing a buzzing sound. He went out to find that an entire swarm had taken up residency and were busily flying in and out of the hive.

Donning his brand new protective gear, he carefully approached the hive from the side and took off the lid. With meticulous care to assure that nobody got crushed, he removed one frame from the top box. It was covered in the exact Italian Honey Bees that he had been planning to purchase! Of course, he had only planned to purchase a starter colony of a couple thousand bees and this swarm appeared closer to 30,000 strong. Score!

So that's a big win for Dave and a little loss for me. I think the balance still works out in our favor!

I still don't know where the money's coming from, but I won't let that stop me from moving forward with my dreams. There's a persistent vision in my mind insisting upon becoming reality – my tree house.

We have the trees and that's a good start. I've also contacted a local tree house architect to start discussing my vision and just what it's going to take to truly build my dream. This is going to be a long-term project but the results will be nothing less than absolutely magical.

Transformation
Monday, May 28, 2018

Our property has completely transformed in the last two weeks. The excavator has come and gone and we now have a gloriously wide open FLAT space in which to move around and make our plans. The driveway has been widened for easy approach and we've got 30+ tons of gravel arriving tomorrow morning. Plus, we now have a sturdy 6'x8' utility shed, thanks to the very generous construction assistance of my sister and her husband.

This morning we met with David of Wild Tree Woodworks to walk the property and assess potential sites for a tree house. We have so many trees, but the trick is finding a small grouping that is spaced and configured to form a good base between them. Then there's the road and the neighbors to consider.

So we've chosen the location for the tree house with a deck over-looking the mossy maple grove. David took lots of measurements and provided me with a design sketch to get started. It'll take a while to save up the money we'll need to build, but until then we have that area on reserve for our tree house of the future.

The next step for The Refuge is having hundreds of feet of trench-es dug; from transformer to shed, and shed to RV utility posts. Then the electrician comes in to lay conduit and wiring, before the electric company comes out to connect the wires, and the county inspector comes to sign off. Oh, and we'll be getting the high-speed broadband wiring installed in there at some point too.

And once all of THAT is done in a month or so… we'll be sitting pretty on our level gravel pads surrounded by forest, enjoying smoking fast internet and unlimited power no matter how cloudy it gets!

Step by little step, The Refuge is beginning to grow…

Holding Pattern
Saturday, June 16, 2018

Should the moat be populated with crocodiles or sharks? It's a crucial decision, since the entrance really sets the tone for a home.

More than four hundred feet of wide-open trenches temporarily decorate the The Refuge while we await the arrival of the next set of contractors. A recent rainstorm deposited enough puddles in the two-feet deep canal that I've declared it a moat.

Accessing our homes from the driveway now requires hopping over the obstacle. I've managed to avoid falling into the hole so far, but Dave hasn't been so lucky.

We're back to the waiting game. Can't do anything else until the wiring is installed, inspected, and approved so the open trenches can be back-filled. Access to my gardening projects is blocked by mounds of dirt, so I'm pretty much stuck.

More gravel is needed to cover the bare dirt that becomes thick mud in the rain, but there's no point in paying for materials now that will just get churned under in the back-fill later.

I have an interview scheduled next week for a job that would be perfect for me. It's only 15 minutes from home, 30 hours per week (how civilized!), and at the heart of the local community. I've been sending out resumes for a lot of different positions, but this one is definitely my favorite possibility. My experience and strengths are a great match for what they need, so here's hoping!

As much as I want all the elements of my life to be in place already, I keep reminding myself to appreciate the stage that we're in now. This is a wild adventure with wide open potential and we've just barely begun to build a home and a life here.

There's a sense of urgency driving me forward, compelling me to manifest this vision at top speed. There's also the sense of immense gratitude that good fortune and my own choices have carried me to this point in life, and I'm equally compelled to appreciate each moment as it unfolds.

I'm edgy with impatience and the suspense of watching my own life progress. What comes next? Do I get the great job and settle into a new lifestyle of relative security? Will the county inspector deny approval for my electricity, requiring more time and money? Do I continue sending out resumes farther and farther from home, accepting the inevitability of a dreaded commute?

All I can do is wait and see...

Fear, Money, and Veggies
Wednesday, July 11, 2018

Rejection always hurts, no matter what form it takes. When that rejection is tied to your ability to continue paying bills and eating... it really turns up the emotional volume. After another round of two interviews for another promising local job, my hopes have been raised and dashed once more.

We're not in dire financial straits yet, but y'all know how I love my advance planning and my plans clearly show the money running out sooner than later without an imminent infusion of steady income. Panic and desperation are each vying for my attention and my faith in the wisdom of this gigantic crazy leap of mine is being tested.

One of the most valuable lessons I've learned along this journey is to avoid making decisions based in fear. That's hard to do when fear is breathing down my neck, but **I know with absolute 100% certainty that fear-based choices do not lead to manifesting my dreams.**

My best option is to continue following my heart into the bold choices it insists upon and to draw on every ounce of courage I can muster to sustain myself through the process. My heart wants a job where my unique talents are necessary and valued. I need a job that needs ME, not just any random body.

The good news is that we're not going to starve. Our recently planted veggie garden is growing exuberantly with all the recent sunshine and our diligent watering and we'll soon be awash in tomatoes and zucchini. The cucumbers and squash aren't far behind,

261

and it looks like we'll even get a handful of strawberries.

I've wanted to grow my own veggies for so long, but I've never had a good space to do it so now I can't wait to take that first juicy bite of my very own home-grown produce!!

We're still waiting for installation of electrical wiring and the open trenches continue slicing and dicing our landscape. Once power and broadband internet are installed, that will open up opportunities for remote jobs. I'm doing my best to keep the faith that everything we need will unfold in good time.

My life is truly amazing and there is no way I could have imagined where I am today from where I was three years ago. All is well and will continue getting better with time.

I just need to keep making choices with my heart...

EPIC
Friday, July 13, 2018

I feel like the Evel Knievel of major life choices – a daredevil risking big leaps over and over. I launched myself at full speed away from a stable career, soaring across a gaping two-year-wide canyon of unemployment and unknown future.

Holding my breath in suspense as I was barely coasting on a breeze with no good landing in sight... and then... finally my feet hit the ground. I made it!

It's my profound pleasure to announce that I begin my new job next week. Drawing on my skills of organization, planning, and communication, I'll be coordinating operations for the local Civic Center.

This non-profit organization is at the heart of the local community and so I'll really be jumping into the deep end of the Key Peninsula. Not only will I get to continue honing my skills and learning new things, but I'll get to meet all sorts of amazing neighbors at the same time. So much goodness all wrapped up in one tidy package!

I'm sure this position will come with the challenges inherent in working with any organization, but I'm refreshed and invigorated and ready to handle anything that comes my way. I enter this next chapter of my life knowing that I have the proven ability to make awesome things happen and I fully intend to continue wielding that power.

It's hard for me to comprehend the undeniable fact that I have transformed my life into exactly what I want it to be. There have been so many choices along the way – points where I could have turned back or taken another path when the road ahead looked too scary.

Each time I found myself with what seemed like a hard decision to make, I recognized one safe option (motivated by fear) and one exhilarating option (motivated by heart.) Taking the heart path every time lead to where I am today.

With this job, I'll achieve both the financial and lifestyle sustainability that are my goals. Those life choices I mentioned before have left me mortgage-free, rent-free, and debt-free. I can support myself with income from only thirty hours per week, and I can even continue slowly investing in our homestead.

My commute will be less than fifteen minutes and only four days per week, leaving me time to devote to the rest of my projects. Being in the center of the community, I'll have lots of chances to make connections with other locals and really grow my roots into the area.

I feel like I've finally arrived home. I've made it. I now have everything I need to continue building the future I envision. My mind continues to be filled with new inspiration even as my dreams are coming true all around me.

This life is already epic and it only gets better from here!

Debutante
Saturday, July 28, 2018

Last weekend I made my debut upon the local high society at the hippest hangout in town. In this community, the wine bar is the happening place to be on Friday nights.

As the new kid in town, I jumped at the opportunity when a member of the Board of Directors (my employers) offered to host my drinks and introduce me around at the popular weekly event. It was a party atmosphere and most of the attendees appeared to be long-time friends and associates. People brought things like cookies, fruits, and cheese to share at the bar with everyone; and local art for sale adorned the walls.

For two hours I sampled a variety of very tasty wines and met every individual in the room. Then I met at least as many people out back in the garden. I met entrepreneurs, artists, professors, travelers, adventurers, and lots of other really interesting folks. I enjoyed great conversations and made a lot of valuable connections.

Everyone was warm, friendly, and genuine; and I felt truly welcomed to the community. And the experience was also utterly exhausting.

If you've been following my journey for very long, you probably know that my need for solitude is far greater than my need for company no matter how much I love connecting with people. It doesn't take long for my social meter to read FULL when in a large group, and then my stamina quickly fades.

But I was really enjoying this gathering of my new community and so I just kept pouring energy into making authentic connections with each introduction. I departed the gathering with an honest smile still on my face, but as I neared the sanctuary of my car I felt the exhaustion suddenly descend.

It reminded me of a facial exercise we did in an acting class long ago: happy face... sad face... happy face... sad face. The light of my dazzling "I'm delighted to be here" smile dimmed to darkness and my whole face sank deep into an ominous frown.

My social meter had overfilled well past the danger mark and was sending off threatening sparks. My growling stomach protested that dinner had been postponed too long. My mood plummeted with unmet needs as I made the short drive home. (Confessions of an Introvert: The Hidden Costs of Staying at the Party.)

When I got home, Dave patiently and kindly listened to me rage on about nothing in particular for about half an hour while I vented all the pent up social stress. My pleasure to meet all of those new people was honest and real, but at the same time I was repressing my need to be alone and away from the crowd.

Life keeps reminding me that there are consequences to repressing my feelings in any given moment and my little post-party temper tantrum was the result of failing to address my needs when I felt them.

I chose this community for a lot of reasons, and one of those reasons is a population small enough to develop a web of one-on-one relationships. I know that the social stress of community gatherings will lessen for me over time. I threw myself into the deep end of the social pool with my new job, knowing that the best way to acclimate is to jump right in.

Being social is most stressful with strangers, but I have the power to change that situation slowly over time. So as hard as it was, I took that first step toward transforming strangers into friends.

Comparative Luxury
Friday, August 17, 2018

My life is getting more luxurious every day. Don't get me wrong... I still limit myself to three-minute showers and I still can't make toast in the morning without burning gasoline, but this lifestyle is providing different kinds of luxuries.

The harvest season is upon us and we've got edibles growing all over the place. For (former) city dwellers like myself, the fact that food literally just springs up out of the ground is really quite magical. Dirt, water, sun, seed... and poof! You've transformed the elements into a tasty fresh salad. How cool is that??

All those huckleberry bushes that I was so excited about when we got this property are now covered in tiny little berries. I've been going out in the morning to pluck the sweetest ripest berries from the bush that's right outside my window and then making fresh huckleberry waffles. Now that's the kind of luxury I'm talking about!

I'm also enjoying the luxury of time. In my former life of arriving at the office before 7am, I could never dream of making waffles before work. My mornings were a model of efficiency with no room for such luxury. I still get up around 5:30am every day, but now I wake naturally and go about my leisurely morning routine with no concern of being late for my 10am start time. (I even wrote this blog before work!)

The four-day work week is also a winner. By the time I'm feeling ready for the week to be over... the week is over. Every weekend is a three-day weekend, which leaves me refreshed and ready to face the world again. "Monday" no longer conjures feelings of dread because I'm enjoying the luxury of better work/life balance.

I've finally gotten around to making the interior space of my home, my own. Gone is all of the original RV furniture that was uncomfortable and didn't really suit my needs. Now my space is tailored to me with a functional office area including lots of storage, and a comfortable lounge area with more storage and a much better view of the TV. Finally, the luxury of watching a movie in comfort!

When I lived in the city, my choice of pets was very limited by my homeowners' association. But here, we have the luxury of adopting a rooster on a whim, just like we did last weekend. The rooster (who now answers to the name Brick) has a comfy nest in Dave's garage, but he roams freely around the property most of the day. He's a sweet boy, and likes to come to my doorstep clucking softly, just to say hi when I get home from work.

After more than two months of open trenches, our electrical and broadband wiring were finally installed this week and the land has been restored to its former flatness. There is light at the end of the tunnel... and soon it's going to turn on at the flip of a switch! By the end of this month, we should be fully hooked into grid power. Wohoo!

And then... I can add gasoline-free toast to my growing list of comparative luxuries.

Sanctuary
Wednesday, August 29, 2018

The Refuge is now an official Backyard Wildlife Sanctuary as ordained by the Washington Department of Fish and Wildlife. Our home is not only our personal retreat from the outside world, but also a purposeful haven for the creatures who inhabited this land before we arrived.

We've gotten to know the family of deer who make an appearance almost daily. The mama doe and her two fawns still approach our clearing with all due caution, but they're content to graze while we watch them from nearby. Dave put a salt lick along their usual path to encourage them to return often.

While watering my garden I noticed a tree frog hop out to perch on a big leaf. I gave him a gentle spray of droplets and then moved onto the next container, where a second little froggy jumped out to the edge. And then it happened

again! I had accidentally created the perfect frog habitat with big leafy plants and damp shady soil. Now they sing their croaky frog songs to me most evenings.

Just outside my big picture windows are elderberry and hazelnut trees, and lots of huckleberry bushes. I was really looking forward to eating fresh hazelnuts, but the blue jays made it clear that they weren't willing to share as they plucked every last pod from among the leaves. At least I got to enjoy the show as those vividly blue bodies darted in and out to snatch their treasures.

I never did get to taste the elderberries either, but I got to witness so many species of birds coming to enjoy the harvest. Fortunately, there are still more than enough huckleberries to feed me and all the local wildlife. Even our resident rooster will happily take a huckleberry from my hand.

The application process for becoming a Backyard Wildlife Sanctuary was pretty simple, but it did include a fairly extensive questionnaire about wildlife conservation practices on our land. It was educational about the need to keep snag trees (dead wood), bramble patches, debris piles, and other "less attractive" natural habitats for so many creatures. It also helped to guide us in how we want to develop the land in the future.

The need for wild animals to access water was stressed, so our plans will include little streams and ponds. The questionnaire was also a reminder that leaving plenty of space for weeds and wild growth supports the wildlife better than a big manicured lawn. Adding bird houses, bat houses, squirrel houses, and anything else that we come up with will encourage the locals to flock here and thrive.

The designation as a Backyard Wildlife Sanctuary doesn't carry any weight beyond that pretty sign now hanging at our entrance, but it announces one of our primary values – respecting the land and the life on it. It states our intention to protect and care for Nature.

And just in case the rumors are true about owls being well-educated... they can read the sign and know that they're welcome here.

Power
Monday, September 10, 2018

Power is one of those things that you never truly value until it's gone. It's out of mind until you flip a switch and nothing happens. Our society tends to consume energy voraciously without conscious thought, but I've lived a very different lifestyle for the past fourteen months.

When we first started boondocking, I relied sparingly on my gasoline generator for everything except the lights. Things like turning on the TV or recharging my laptop required burning fossil fuel. When we arrived in the Arizona desert – one of the sunniest places in the USA – I made the investment in solar panels and all the other necessary components to convert sunshine into energy.

Solar power was a definite upgrade, causing none of the noise, air pollution, or expense of the gasoline generator. But the sun does disappear at night and is greatly reduced on cloudy days. My power was still inconsistent and very limited, requiring strategic living.

In this lifestyle, I've become conscious of all the resources I consume. I've come to understand how much power it takes to boil water in my electric kettle, and how much sun my panels will need to refill my batteries afterwards. I've learned that turning off my propane-fueled fridge at night saves resources while still maintaining cold. Even when I use "connected" faucets now, it's become habit to use only a trickle of water for washing.

But as great as it's been to learn how to live with less... I'm ready for more again. It is my great joy to announce that The Refuge is now connected to unlimited power 24/7. All hail the grid!

I just plugged in my RV for the first time in fourteen months and it feels awesome. I celebrated by switching the fridge from propane to electric operation. Then I went wild and ran the crock pot for several hours. We really know how to party around here!

Much like getting the land cleared and leveled, achieving grid power is a major development milestone. These improvements to the property make a significant impact on quality of life. Very soon we'll also have broadband internet turned on, which will be another big leap in the direction of comfort and convenience.

The leaves are starting to turn brown and fall from the trees, hinting at an early Autumn. The ground will soon be saturated with rainfall again, increasing the difficulty of installing the well and septic system that we need.

Time is of the essence, but contractors and finances have yet to solidify into a workable plan. The County hasn't approved the septic design, and I don't know how we're going to pay for it yet anyway. Winter is coming and I don't feel very prepared.

The path forward from this point isn't clear to me yet. I've enjoyed the security of paying cash for everything so far, but my financial power is now as depleted as solar energy in the gray Northwest winter. I dearly want to continue living debt-free, but continuing this project – making the property livable – is just going to take a lot more cash than we have available.

So I'm thinking about taking the huge leap of applying for a construction loan to build an actual on-the-grid, "sticks and bricks" house. Water and septic systems would be an assumed cost rolled into a construction loan, taking care of that problem. Plus, as an added bonus... a house!

Of course, a loan would mean embracing decades of monthly payments (and oh, how I loathe paying interest), but it would also be a solid investment in so many ways. It could even be a self-sustaining investment if we choose to rent out the brand new house instead of living in it.

I don't know. Maybe I'm drunk on power and just dreaming about how to get more and more, but dreaming is what started this whole adventure in the first place...

A Beginning
Wednesday, October 03, 2018

Every ending is a new beginning, and I have another one just dawning over the horizon. In my last blog I shared that my dreams have turned to building a house on my land. With the generous assistance of my parents, that dream can now become reality.

Before I started Project Retreat Forward, I had all the comforts of home and city dwelling easily available, even though I didn't feel any true joy or satisfaction in my daily living. As I began the Project, I set out to change my life without having any real idea of what else my life could be. Nonetheless, I was committed to finding the authentic joy and satisfaction that I'd been missing.

Before the Project, the security of a well-paying job; a nice comfortable home; plenty of good people in my life... it just didn't feel like enough. On Maslow's Hierarchy of Needs, I had the basics of Food and Rest; Security and Safety; and Belonging and Love covered. What I lacked were those upper hierarchy feelings of Accomplishment, and of Achieving Potential.

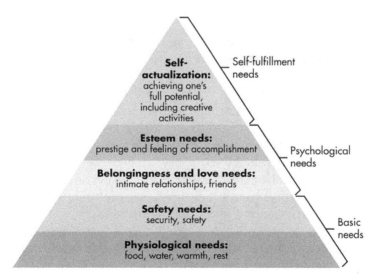

In the course of changing my life, my choices included the painful and difficult process of removing myself from every comfort and security – leaving my sole source of income, my home, my family and communities behind. I set off on an adventure of ultimate free-

271

dom, traveling anywhere in the world that my heart desired. My experiences earned me stories that I'll be telling for the rest of my life and left me feeling that I've achieved something worthwhile.

Looking back, I see that I abandoned my well-covered basic Needs in a quest to meet my higher Needs. Now that I feel I've Accomplished my wildest imaginings over these last few years, I'm compelled to improve on those basic needs of Shelter and Security that I minimized for the journey.

And just like my travels took me full circle around the world, my internal journey has taken me from security to free-wheeling adventure and is now circling back toward security again. This period of growth feels complete, having allowed me to roam freely to my heart's content and then create a solid foundation upon which to construct my future.

Time to build a house!

With this blog, Project Retreat Forward officially concludes. This part of my story has reached its natural ending.

The heroine rescued herself from too much civilization, and after many amazing adventures, now lives happily among the trees with her handsome prince and an ever-growing assortment of animals.

Of course, life goes on. The Refuge and our challenges in homestead building will continue, but that begins a new story.

I plan to continue Retreating Forward as my guiding philosophy in life. I've learned that meeting my own needs allows me to be my best self in relation to the world and everyone else in it. I've learned that listening to my feelings helps me make good choices. I've learned to trust in my own inner compass.

Thank you for being part of my journey, for your thoughts and good wishes, and simply for caring.

Go forth into the unknown and live your dreams, my friends!